A Teacher's Guide to Supporting Gifted Middle School Students

T0386587

A Teacher's Guide to Supporting Gifted Middle School Students provides insight to help you gain a better understanding of your gifted students during a pivotal time in their development.

Employing pop culture, personal stories, and prompts for reflection, this text considers major factors impacting gifted middle school students including self-image, the need for differentiated content, the importance of slowing down, the value of mentors, and ways to instill hope during this – more often than not – difficult time. Full of practical examples for how you can work to address both the academic and social-emotional needs of your students, this book champions middle school as an important time for self-discovery and developing passions.

Engaging and informative, this inspiring new book is a "must read" for all teachers seeking to positively influence their students during this unique and critical time in their lives.

DJ Graham is Principal of the Gary K. Herberger Young Scholars Academy, a middle and high school for gifted learners in Phoenix, Arizona. He provides insights, experience, and guidance as a speaker at state and national education conferences, focusing on the social-emotional and academic needs of gifted adolescents and integrating pop culture into the curriculum.

A Teacher's Guide to Supporting Gifted Middle School Students

Reaching Adolescents in the Pivotal Years

DJ Graham

Routledge
Taylor & Francis Group

NEW YORK AND LONDON

Cover image credit: © Getty Images

First published 2023
by Routledge
605 Third Avenue, New York, NY 10158

and by Routledge
4 Park Square, Milton Park, Abingdon, Oxon, OX14 4RN

Routledge is an imprint of the Taylor & Francis Group, an informa business

Library of Congress Cataloging-in-Publication Data
Names: Graham, DJ, author.
Title: A teacher's guide to supporting gifted middle school students :
reaching adolescents in the pivotal years / DJ Graham.
Description: First Edition. | New York : Routledge, 2023. |
Includes bibliographical references. |
Identifiers: LCCN 2022046780 (print) | LCCN 2022046781 (ebook) |
ISBN 9781032364490 (Hardback) | ISBN 9781032363684 (Paperback) |
ISBN 9781003332015 (eBook)
Subjects: LCSH: Gifted children–Education (Middle school) |
Middle school teaching–United States–Anecdotes. | Teacher-student relationships. |
Mentoring in education. | Individualized instruction. | Identity (Psychology) |
Perfectionism (Personality trait)
Classification: LCC LC3993.23 .G73 2023 (print) |
LCC LC3993.23 (ebook) | DDC 371.95/73–dc23/eng/20221230
LC record available at https://lccn.loc.gov/2022046780
LC ebook record available at https://lccn.loc.gov/2022046781

ISBN: 978-1-032-36449-0 (hbk)
ISBN: 978-1-032-36368-4 (pbk)
ISBN: 978-1-003-33201-5 (ebk)

DOI: 10.4324/9781003332015

Typeset in Optima
by Newgen Publishing UK

This book is dedicated to my wife, Lea, and my daughter, Gwen.

Lea – You have always believed in me and my dreams, and I can never thank you enough. This book would never have been finished without you.

Gwen – You bring me so much joy, and I want this book to inspire you to always follow your own dreams.

Contents

Acknowledgments

This book would not be possible without the guidance, influence, and support of the following people:

My mother, Pamela Graham, for being my educational hero and helping me to be the teacher I am today.

My father, David Graham, for always believing I could achieve anything.

My mother-in-law, Lilly Soto, for giving me the opportunity to finish this book.

Dina Brulles, for being an amazing mentor who has guided and provided me with so many opportunities.

Randi Posner who accepted a student teacher years ago and set my whole career in motion.

Kimberly Lansdowne and Michael Twilling – you have both shown me what it means to be a leader for gifted students.

Amanda Binder and Lainie Seretis – I learned so much working with the two of you, and value our time building such a special program for gifted middle schoolers.

Finally, every student I have had the pleasure of teaching. You have all had an impact on my life, and I cannot thank you enough. Your enthusiasm and drive inspire me, and I hope you see yourselves within the pages of this book.

Meet the Author

DJ Graham is Principal of the Gary K. Herberger Young Scholars Academy, a middle and high school for gifted learners in Phoenix, Arizona. He has more than a decade of experience in the field of gifted education, teaching and developing curriculum. DJ provides insights, experience, and guidance as a speaker at state and national education conferences, focusing on the social-emotional and academic needs of gifted adolescents and integrating pop culture into the curriculum. He obtained master's degrees in Gifted Education Curriculum & Instruction and Educational Administration from Arizona State University and Grand Canyon University respectively. DJ is currently a doctoral student at Northern Arizona University, pursuing a degree in Educational Leadership.

Foreword

These simple words, "I teach middle schoolers," can make people cringe. Add "gifted" to those words, and many just shake their heads in wonderment. Gifted middle school students are a unique group to teach. They can be exhilaratingly fun, frustrating, and formidable all within the same class period. DJ Graham's sensitivity toward these students is the jumping-off point in this book where he provides a fresh and somewhat comforting perspective on how teachers can begin to understand and relate to the rapidly maturing, brilliant, and often quirky learners we call gifted middle schoolers.

Throughout the text, Graham ingrains commonly misunderstood traits of many middle school gifted learners. He helps teachers understand how to embrace and build on those traits and sometimes challenging behaviors, such as asynchronous development, underachievement, twice-exceptionality, a heightened sense of justice, perfectionism, overexcitabilities, and so many other nuanced characteristics. He speaks from experience. These traits and characteristics are all embedded into the practical advice he offers and the learning experiences he shares while also being supported by research and best practices in gifted education.

As the gifted coordinator for the school district where DJ taught gifted programs, I had the unique opportunity of watching him teach in a variety of settings: first, as a student teacher in a gifted cluster classroom when his teacher mentor beckoned me to observe this brilliant young teacher who connected naturally and intuitively with his gifted students; and then on numerous occasions later while he was teaching in the specialized gifted middle school program for highly gifted learners. I observed the ease with which he connected with his students, the insights he routinely made, and the earnest compassion he demonstrated for his students.

Teaching as a substitute teacher in his former classroom last year during the teacher shortage caused by the pandemic, I felt firsthand the trepidation many teachers feel when teaching gifted middle school students. Through this book, DJ Graham expertly guides readers in navigating and appreciating this unique teaching experience.

While all authors build on their personal experiences, DJ leads the reader in both understanding and supporting these learners – both through the eyes of a former gifted middle school student who struggled with similar issues and as a teacher who used his experiences to shape his students' learning. Guided by personal reflections and experiences, he makes you feel comfortable in your discomfort about teaching and working with gifted middle schoolers. He accomplishes this feat by showing how enthusiasm and passion infuse learning and help to coalesce students with their teachers, engulfing the students in the freedom to explore, question, argue, and defend their constantly emerging and fluid ideas.

To engage reluctant learners, clearly a common concern when teaching gifted middle schoolers, Graham demonstrates how to intermix curriculum with the students' "real-world" connections; that is, current events, superheroes, cartoon figures, and pop culture *du jour*. This is his way of saying that to connect with them you must relate to them.

Graham evokes the poignant, personal, and sometimes painful thoughts these students may be experiencing. He shows how to draw in students to become comfortable in their learning by masterfully embedding a plethora of references to current media, highlighting movies, TV shows, songs, literature, video, audio, etc. The message comes across to the students as accepting, inviting, and reassuring. Students realize they are not alone; there is an abundance of connections they can make.

Our gifted middle schoolers feel safe and understood when their teachers see and relate to them in the ways discussed in this book, reflecting the lived experiences of the author. In almost a subliminal undercurrent, DJ imbues the importance of building community, a classroom culture, and a feeling of acceptance, support, and belonging – a calming thought during the turbulent times of a gifted adolescent.

This book is an insider's guide to teaching gifted middle schoolers. The book fills a gap in a unique, thoughtful, and sensitive way. Graham's words do not cast blame on those of us who have not lived his or his students' experiences. Instead, they shine light on what we may have missed in teacher certification programs and other professional learning opportunities.

I have sat beside DJ in parent meetings, student meetings, administrative meetings, and Arizona State University meetings where we both teach in the master's degree program in Gifted Education. He understands this group of students at an unparalleled level in my experience. I feel honored to share with you my perspective on his thoughts and experiences. My hope is that you can influence your students and others by sharing his messages and insights.

Dina Brulles, PhD, Gifted Program Coordinator,
Arizona State University, and former Director of Gifted Education in
Paradise Valley Unified School District, Arizona

Introduction

If there is one thing you take away from this book, I want it to be this: middle school is hard.

Before you rush to Amazon to see if you are still in the window to return this book, think about who you were in middle school. What were you like? What were your interests? Who were your friends? What were your dreams? When I look back at this time in my life, it is not with favor.

Although I did not have a bad experience, it was not great either. I was a gifted adolescent who felt incredibly awkward, trying to strike a balance between doing well in school while still appearing cool (I was not particularly good at this one). I was embarrassed that I still played Pokémon cards but did not want to give up something I loved. Each day was filled with the worry that my peers would notice my acne. While I earned good grades, I was not challenged, and I felt lost as English, my favorite subject, stopped being the greatest time of the day. I dreamed of being a published author. Every day on the bus ride home, I would tell my friend about my ideas for books, and felt mortified when they said they did not want to hear about them anymore and wanted to talk about something else.

My experience is not that uncommon. When I started working with gifted middle schoolers, I taught in a self-contained program. My first day, I stood in front of a room full of kids who were just like me when I was their age, and we were all nervous. They were a group trying to figure out who they were going to be at this new school. I was their teacher, trying to figure out how to make their experience better than my own.

DOI: 10.4324/9781003332015-1

You Teach Middle School? I'm Sorry!

When I tell people I work with middle schoolers, their reactions tend to be similar. Many will express disbelief, not sure how I deal with so many adolescents every day. Others share how much they hated middle school and never want to go back. The most extreme response was somebody who said, "You teach middle school? I'm sorry!"

I understand their point of view. Middle school is a time of massive changes, with newfound freedoms that can be just as detrimental as they are empowering. Relationships (both romantic and platonic) become a priority, and bonds that seemed strong can be broken. School becomes more challenging, and, to top it all off, adolescents' bodies are going through massive physical changes.

Searching on the phrase "Middle School Survival Guide" on Amazon yields ten different book results addressed at helping kids navigate middle school (there were more that included general advice for teens, but I limited it only to those focused on middle school). Searching on the same phrase on YouTube presents more than 50 videos identified as "survival guides" for middle school. Even Nickelodeon had a show, *Ned's Declassified School Survival Guide*, which ran from 2004–2007 and was set at a middle school (Fellows, n.d.). For so many people, middle school is not just something you get through, but rather, something you must survive.

While this time is a challenge for all kids, for gifted students, this time can be even more confusing. In addition to the normal challenges that adolescents face, being gifted adds a completely different set of academic and social-emotional challenges. One of the common traits of gifted students is asynchronous development, where a gifted child's development is essentially out of sync (Webb, 2016). In certain areas the student is processing and reasoning ahead of their same-age peers, but in other areas, they are emotionally in line with or behind those same peers (Silverman, 1997). This can be confusing, frustrating, and cause problems, as students try to manage this disjointed development

On top of all these internal changes, the entire structure of school itself changes with the shift from elementary to middle. Instead of having one class where students learn all their content, they now have multiple classes, which means understanding several different sets of expectations, routines, and social dynamics. In many instances, what is valued in middle school changes as does what it means to be successful (Besnoy et al., 2011). This can cause gifted students to doubt their abilities, and, in some cases, results in underachievement (Besnoy et al., 2011). These students have enormous potential, yet this is an incredibly fragile time.

The Goals of This Book

For this book, I have two primary goals. First, I want to provide an understanding of who our gifted middle schoolers are. I have been fortunate to teach this grade level for more than a decade, and each day, I find new things that make me smile. This is an age group that can have an in-depth discussion about chemistry that will leave you in awe, while also giggling at the word "duty." They are members of a group who are looking for understanding, and this time can feel incredibly lonely. This time period is so important, and even by just understanding their perspective we can go a long way in supporting them.

Second, I want to empower you in supporting your gifted students. This field is one that has many misconceptions and misunderstandings, and I have met and worked with many teachers who are desperate to help their gifted learners. They just want the tools to do it. My goal is for you to be able to finish each chapter and have a deeper understanding of your gifted students along with specific strategies and examples you can directly apply in the classroom. I also structure this book for book study use. Broken into ten parts, starting in August, one chapter can be addressed each month throughout a traditional school year. This allows time to reflect on each concept, while also applying different strategies for your unique setting. Regardless of how you use it, I want the concepts and strategies to be meaningful to your classroom.

The Structure

While I was fortunate to have a very positive experience in my college education classes, it was not until experiencing my internships and student teaching that all the lessons from my courses really clicked. Watching teachers directly interact with students and hearing their insights about what went well and what could be improved upon were more valuable than any book chapter I read while attaining my undergraduate degree. Although the theories and research were foundational, I did not truly understand what they meant until experiencing it. I noticed something similar when I first started presenting on gifted education. While citing journal articles and experts from the field was important, the most impactful parts of any session I taught were the reflection and sharing of my experiences, essentially bringing to life what the theory looked like in actual practice.

As I considered how to structure this book, those lessons had a major influence on what you are about to read. Everything within this text is built on the research and experiences of experts within the field, but to bring that to life, I have intertwined my own experiences working with gifted middle schoolers. My hope is that these examples will help not only to make the research come to life, but also you will see yourself in the examples presented.

Another element of this book touches on who I am as a teacher. I *love* pop culture, and it was one of the quickest ways I found to connect to my gifted middle schoolers. Talking about video games, movies, comic books, and music was the way I forged small connections with my students that would make the class much more comfortable. Eventually I saw opportunities to exemplify the lessons I was teaching, bridging what they already knew with the standards they needed to learn. These lessons were some of my students' favorites, and eventually I started integrating pop culture into my professional development presentations as well. Sprinkled throughout this book you will see references to various movies, music, and television shows. While some are fun connections to a concept or an idea, my hope is that they will serve as anchors for you to connect with each concept.

Finally, this book is designed for all middle school teachers to gain a better understanding of their gifted students and how they can support them. Chapter 1 provides an overview of the characteristics of gifted learners. There are many misconceptions that come with being identified as "gifted," and before we can work to support our students, we need to better understand them. This chapter also discusses identifying gifted students. While testing is usually performed in elementary school, understanding the traits and characteristics of gifted students is important for providing appropriate support. In addition, even if a student is not formally identified, that does not mean we cannot work to provide them with an enriching environment that can meet their needs.

Chapters 2, 3, and 4 are each focused on the concept of culture building and how gifted students see and understand themselves. Chapter 2 begins by exploring the significance of identity development for adolescents, as well as the role culture plays in supporting this stage of life. In addition, strategies for creating a positive classroom culture are shared. Chapter 3 focuses on an element of self-image that impacts many gifted students: perfectionism. The characteristics are shared, as well as ways teachers can work to help students understand the value in making mistakes. Chapter 4 builds on the previous two chapters and focuses primarily on practical ways teachers can help students in developing their identities. Through a meaningful use of our assignments and the ways we interact with our classes, gifted middle schoolers can not only feel comfortable being who they are, but also take risks in exploring and developing their identities.

Chapters 5, 6, and 7 shift from social-emotional development to content. Chapter 5 provides the foundational understanding of the elements of differentiation. While this concept is used with English language learners and in special education classrooms, it is also the key to supporting gifted students. Through this chapter, an understanding of each element is provided, as well as how it applies to gifted learners. Furthermore, the elements themselves are considered specifically for middle school classrooms. Chapter 6 continues the understanding of differentiation and focuses on how teachers can adjust their curriculum with consideration for student readiness, learning profiles, and interests. Chapter 7 is a culmination of both preceding chapters and focuses on providing examples of what differentiation looks like within a classroom. Utilizing two different assignments, lesson plans are provided with my commentary, explaining why choices were made and how individual elements represent differentiation.

The final section of the book returns to explore social-emotional aspects of being a gifted middle schooler. Chapter 8 considers the role time plays in the lives of our students, and the ways in which we can support them. First, the roles of grading and homework are important considerations for how our students use their time, and the ways we utilize these elements are discussed. In addition, the chapter considers the delicate balance gifted middle schoolers are trying to strike, with oncoming adulthood and the last remnants of childhood. As teachers, we play an important role in supporting our students in understanding it is alright to have fun.

Chapter 9 explores mentorships, one of the strategies recommended for supporting gifted students. Through a consideration of strategies that can be implemented in any class, as well as considerations for designing a formal mentorship program, the ways in which we can support our gifted middle schoolers through experiences are discussed. Chapter 10 closes out the book with a clear thesis: middle school is hard and, sometimes, there is nothing that can be done to avoid that. In realizing this challenge, this chapter discusses the role we play in guiding and supporting our students through this difficult time.

Reflection

Every chapter will end with reflection prompts for you to consider what you have read. While you are welcome to write your responses to the questions, they are designed for discussion and consideration of our practice as teachers. I know it is tempting to want to skip the questions at the end of a chapter, but I ask that you at least think about each prompt, as they will either help frame what was discussed or help prepare for the upcoming chapter. For the Introduction, please consider the following prompts:

1. What was your experience in middle school like? Do you look back fondly or do you wish you could forget that time? What do you wish a teacher had done to make it better?
2. What are your goals with this book?

References

Besnoy, K. D., Jolly, J. L., & Manning, S. (2011). Academic underachievement of gifted students. In J. A. Castellano & A. D. Frazier (Eds.), *Special populations in gifted education: Understanding our most able students from diverse backgrounds* (pp. 401–415). Prufrock Press Inc.

Fellows, S. (Program Creator). (n.d.). *Ned's declassified survival guide* [TV series]. Nickelodeon.

Silverman, L. K. (1997). The construct of asynchronous development. *Peabody Journal of Education*, *72*(3/4), 36–58.

Webb, J. T. (Ed.). (2016). *Misdiagnosis and dual diagnoses of gifted children and adults: ADHD, bipolar, OCD, Asperger's, depression, and other disorders* (2nd ed.). Great Potential Press, Inc.

Lisa Simpson, Calvin, and Spider-Man Walk into a Classroom…

The title of this chapter is not some clever joke, but rather, the experience many teachers have when working with gifted individuals. Each day they are faced with teaching students with varied backgrounds, experiences, and willingness to learn. While trying to juggle meeting all the unique needs of each student, data and clear criteria drive interventions and support. When it comes to gifted students, though, despite the existence of common traits, this population is just as diverse and varied as any other group.

Take the three characters used in the chapter title: Lisa Simpson from *The Simpsons*, Peter Parker from *Spider-Man*, and Calvin from *Calvin and Hobbes*. Each of these characters exhibits traits and characteristics of gift-edness, and, even if they are not formally identified, each has unique needs that need to be addressed.

Lisa is what many people envision when they think of gifted students. She is incredibly intelligent with an aptitude for a variety of subjects. In class, she always has the right answer, and her propensity for being a know-it-all can irritate those around her. She cares deeply about her grades, and the stress of doing well can be overwhelming. She has a strong sense of justice and wants to make the world a better place. Students like Lisa are what make people think that having the "gifted" or "honors" class is easy.

In many ways, Peter Parker is like Lisa. They are both highly intelligent, grasp concepts easily, and the drive to do the right thing can even come at the cost of their own happiness. Unlike Lisa, however, Peter's world out-side of class interferes with his ability to focus on his work, and his grades can suffer as a result. In the 2002 film *Spider-Man 2*, one of Peter's college professors describes him as "smart but lazy" (Raimi, 2004). Students like Peter can be frustrating to work with, but the potential is apparent.

DOI: 10.4324/9781003332015-2

Students like Calvin, though, are not as easily recognizable as gifted. While he does not go unnoticed in class, he is noticed for all the wrong reasons. While his classmate Susie is viewed as the perfect student, Calvin is sarcastic, finds ways out of doing his work, and often spends time in his own imagination. Although his grades are very poor, Calvin is incredibly observant and asks questions in ways well above his age. Students like Calvin sit in classrooms around the country, not having their needs met and falling through the cracks.

The purpose of this chapter is to provide a foundation outlining who our gifted students are, as well as many of the characteristics that are associated with this population. In understanding the characteristics of gifted students, we are better able to provide differentiation and support, while also being able to help find those who might not formally be identified.

Blue and Black or White and Gold?

In 2015, the internet was overtaken with talk of "The Dress," which was just a simple photo of an article of clothing. What grabbed the attention of so many people was that different people perceived the colors differently. Some saw the article of clothing as blue and black, while others (myself included) saw it as white and gold ("The Dress," 2022). Although the science behind it – how so many people could perceive something so differently – is interesting, this is the experience many of our gifted students have. Even though there are established characteristics, I have encountered many individuals who do not fully understand what it means to be gifted. The students whom teachers would assume are gifted have not qualified for gifted services, while those who get pulled out for enrichment shock and surprise the class.

I do not think this is surprising, considering that gifted education is not placed front and center in most teacher preparation programs. Determinations and resources for gifted education are left to the discretion of individual states, and each state has their own definition of what qualifies someone as gifted, as well as whether or not services are required (Rinn et al., 2020). Despite the fact that many of these definitions include similar qualities or attributes, there is still a distinction in how gifted students are supported across the United States.

The National Association for Gifted Children (NAGC) is the national organization designed to support gifted students, their parents, educators, and state gifted organizations. Through different resources including conferences, publications, and an informational website, they have done a great deal to help support this population. One of the ways they have done this is by updating their definition of giftedness in 2019 to focus on understanding what it means to be gifted, not just identification (National Association for Gifted Children, 2019). Below is the updated definition the NAGC uses:

> Students with gifts and talents perform – or have the capability to perform – at higher levels compared to others of the same age, experience, and environment in one or more domains. They require modification(s) to their educational experience(s) to learn and realize their potential. Student with gifts and talents:
>
> - Come from all racial, ethnic, and cultural populations, as well as all economic strata.
> - Require sufficient access to appropriate learning opportunities to realize their potential.
> - Can have learning and processing disorders that require specialized intervention and accommodation.
> - Need support and guidance to develop socially and emotionally as well as in their areas of talent.
> - Require varied services based on their changing needs.
>
> (National Association for Gifted Children, 2019, p. 1)

While this definition is clear, there are elements that stand in contrast to what many people assume "being gifted" means.

Like the perceived coloring of the dress, assuming that gifted students are only those who get perfect grades ignores many students who need support and modifications to their education. As the definition acknowledges, gifted students are not just those who earn perfect grades, but can also be students who require individualized education plans (IEPs) or 504s, are English language learners (ELLs), who underachieve, and come from any background (Castellano & Frazier, 2011). As the definition also highlights, our gifted students do not already have to be performing ahead of their age peers, but rather, have the potential to do so (National Association for Gifted Children, 2019). Our gifted students are just as varied as any other population within our schools and understanding this allows us to better meet their needs.

Common Traits of Gifted Learners

Although the definition from the NAGC is comprehensive, there are specific characteristics it is important to recognize regarding this population. In order to help frame our understanding of gifted students, I have identified five traits you might experience or see in your classrooms. It is also important to note that no two gifted students are exactly alike, and a student might not exhibit a specific trait or it may be less pronounced than others. As you read through this list, I encourage you to reflect on whether you have seen this trait with the gifted students you have taught and how it aligns with the NAGC definition.

Trait 1: Above-Age Intellect, Reasoning, and Curiosity

When people think "gifted," above average intellect and reasoning is often the first thing that comes to mind, and for good reason. In the NAGC report, *2018–2019 State of the States in Gifted Education*, 36 of the documented state definitions for gifted education referenced "advanced intellectual ability" (Rinn et al., 2020). Gifted students as a population tend to be academically ahead of their age peers in one or more areas (Clark, 2002). This is typically the first indication for parents and teachers that their child might require specialized instruction to meet their unique academic needs. For example, students might begin reading at a younger age than their peers, be advanced in their vocabulary and communication, or grasp concepts at a faster rate (Winebrenner & Brulles, 2018).

In addition, many gifted students see relationships between topics, and often bridge gaps that others do not see (Winebrenner & Brulles, 2018). Teaching this population can be so much fun, as the ideas they present can take content into unexpected places. When I am teaching history, my students regularly ask questions I never considered, and shape our class in such a positive way.

It is important to note, however, that this does not mean that they exhibit the same academic talents in every subject. For example, "twice-exceptional" describes students who are gifted yet also have "learning or processing disorders" (National Association for Gifted Children, 2019; Sousa, 2009). This identification can be confusing, if not paradoxical, and can result in issues with students getting identified, as each component has unique needs and characteristics (Sousa, 2009). Despite these differences, the child is gifted, and their strengths are an important aspect of their educational journey (Baldwin et al., 2015).

Also, above average intellect is *not* always reflected in achievement. Gifted students can underachieve, which is where they do not perform at the expected level (Besnoy et al., 2011). Grades often are a reflection of how a student completed an assignment, and, for some gifted students, if they do not see the value in a task or it is a concept they already know, they might not complete it (Winebrenner & Brulles, 2018). This is one of the reasons that assignments must be at the level of complexity that gifted students need.

When considering who our gifted students are, do not just rely on results in a grade book. Instead, look at the way the student thinks about the material, as well as the way they talk about it. At the middle school level, it is common to find gifted students asking complex questions and connecting content to the real world. As a teacher, this is such an exciting thing, as it allows you to dig deeper into curriculum than you might have originally expected. Some of my favorite moments as a teacher were not the lessons I planned, but the unexpected detours we took as a class.

Trait 2: Asynchronous Development

Asynchronous development means gifted children tend to develop in ways that are not consistent. While intellectually they are ahead of their age peers, physically and emotionally they are more in line with their developmental age. This disjointed development can be frustrating, as a 10-year-old gifted child might be reasoning at the age equivalent of a 16 year-old, but emotionally processing that information as a 10 year-old (Silverman, 1997). What makes this even more challenging is that this development is not consistent across content areas and domains, so one child might have several different age levels represented in how they are navigating the world (Silverman, 1997).

Another important consideration with asynchronous development is that this uneven development can result in poor judgment, as intellect and emotional maturity are not aligned (Webb, 2016). For teachers, parents, and students, it can be incredibly confusing and frustrating, as the choices gifted kids make can lack the maturity and forward thinking we would expect them to have. Webb (2016) explains that this lack of judgment is connected to natural brain development, and higher levels of intellect result in a bigger gap in judgment.

Trait 3: Strong Sense of Justice

Gifted students tend to have a very strong sense of right and wrong, and will often call out perceived injustices (Clark, 2002). If a policy or procedure is not fair, gifted students will feel uncomfortable with the situation. While competition can be a motivator for gifted youth, if there are aspects to the game they do not think are fair and just, they will question it. I have seen many classroom review games of Jeopardy! fall apart as gifted students feel the questions they received were unfair or the team composition was not appropriate.

As regards larger societal issues, there can be an added stress where students feel like they need to solve the problems facing the world (Clark, 2002). These feelings can add pressure and stress as they try and solve issues that the world has been facing for years. Issues like inequality can weigh heavily on gifted learners and can feel insurmountable. This is very important to keep in mind, especially when dealing with world issues, as these concerns can weigh heavily on students. Even if your content feels disconnected from what is happening in the world, being aware of the way current events can impact your students is critical.

Trait 4: Creativity

Like intellectual ability, creativity is often connected with gifted education. The *2018–2019 State of the States in Gifted Education* report acknowledged that 31 of the states included "creativity or creative thinking" as part of their definitions (Rinn et al., 2020). In *Understanding Creativity*, Dr. Jane Piitro explains that creativity and gifted education have been linked for decades through various conceptual definitions (2004). This understanding is important, as our creative thinkers can approach the world from unique and amazing perspectives, yet they can struggle in traditional learning environments (Winebrenner & Brulles, 2018). Their perspective and ability to dream up unique and innovative solutions can stand in conflict with the sometimes regimented structure of traditional school environments.

Trait 5: Intensity

Gifted students tend to feel strongly about what they are experiencing. Whether it is passion for a topic they love or pressure from the world around them, they feel it intensely. One of the original core ideas about gifted education was Dabrowski's theory of overexcitabilities (Lind, 2011). The basic concept is related to the ways in which an individual experiences the world, with those experiencing overexcitabilities having a more intense experience. Dabrowski's theory identifies five different areas: psychomotor (intensified levels of movement, competitiveness, impulsivity, and drive), sensual (heightened reaction to senses, including pleasure and displeasure), intellectual (drive for understanding and curiosity), imaginational (propensity toward metaphor and creation), and emotional (deep levels of empathy and feeling) (Lind, 2011; Sousa, 2009). While gifted students can experience multiple overexcitabilities, that does not mean that they exhibit all of them.

These deeper levels of feeling are important to know, as they help frame some of the reactions our gifted students have. Coupled with the other traits discussed in this section, it helps us to understand what our students are experiencing. For example, a student who experiences a sensual overexcitability might be overtaken by the beauty of a painting and want to spend what we perceive as excessive time taking in all it has to offer. These intense feelings are powerful, and something of which we need to be aware.

I want to address the fact that, although this is a common trait associated with gifted education, there has been debate regarding whether there is enough research to support this link (Bishop, 2021). As more research is conducted, our understanding of the relationship between overexcitabilities and giftedness will grow; however, since this concept has been integrated in much of the early understandings of the field, it is important to consider its relationship to gifted education.

Why Is this Useful?

Since there are so many misconceptions about gifted education, it is very helpful to know the various traits and characteristics that are common with this population. Having this awareness means that you will be better equipped to understand the individuals within your classroom, which, for middle school students, is especially important, as adolescents are seeking understanding and validation of their transition into adulthood (Apter, 2009).

Another aspect of knowing the unique characteristics of gifted students is the ability to advocate for them. Even when identified, this population still must battle with the preconceived understandings about what giftedness truly is. I once worked with a great school counselor, who, like many, assumed that being gifted meant a student would earn straight As. When talking to me about the student, the counselor questioned their identification just because they were earning Cs in their classes. I explained some of the commonly assumed myths about gifted students to them, and while they were receptive to the information, this is a challenge many students in this population face. When people do not understand what it means to be gifted, that can result in experiences which are incredibly negative and detrimental.

This coincides with identification, which is one of the biggest challenges facing gifted education. Schools and districts are stretched thin with their resources, and it can be hard for students to receive appropriate services if they are not identified. The problem, however, is that gifted identification is not a perfect system. This is particularly concerning for African-American, Latinx, and Native American gifted students, as these populations are underrepresented in gifted classes (Peters et al., 2019).

One of the sources of this discrepancy is the identification process itself. For many schools, students are tested for gifted services based on recommendations from teachers and parents (Peters et al., 2019). Because only a small portion of students are tested, this process misses out on students who might be gifted. Research has also found that there is bias within some of the tests used to identify students for gifted services (Peters & Engerrand, 2016). The NAGC has acknowledged this concern, and advocated for schools and districts to evaluate testing procedures to be responsive to the needs of underrepresented populations (National Association for Gifted Children, n.d., 2008). Efforts are being made to close this gap, but there is still a great deal of work left to do.

Do We Even Test Here?

Think back to the opening scenario from this chapter and the variety of gifted students presented. There was a high-achieving student, an underachieving student, and one who likely would go unidentified and not supported. They are all gifted, yet, because of their diverse characteristics and needs, they risk not being understood or supported. As with "The Dress," the perceptions teachers have can influence the ways in which they guide the class.

From my experience, identification procedures are not commonly addressed for middle school educators since honors course work is typically not restricted to gifted students. Qualifying for honors classes tend to be achievement based, which can exclude many. In addition, I have seen districts that have policies which guarantee access to honors classes if students have been identified as gifted, but this does not account for those unidentified. By understanding these traits and characteristics, however, we can support our gifted students in receiving the services they need.

Even if there is not a formal identification process at your middle school, by looking for these traits, you can recommend students who might not be identified for honors classes. This will enable them to receive more complex material and be challenged. If a student is not achieving, this challenge can potentially drive them to succeed.

Depending on the school's policies or availability in honors courses, even with a teacher's recommendation, a student might not be admitted to a gifted program. As a result, they will not be receiving services and support they might need. As instructors, we have a great deal of ownership over the curriculum we teach and how we teach it. Meaningful differentiation for gifted learners can occur in our classes even without a formal identification.

Summary

Gifted students are a population met with many preconceived ideas about what the identification means. While there are certain traits most associated with the population, there are others that can be surprising or even frustrating. By understanding the characteristics of gifted learners, educators are better equipped to meet these unique needs, and primed to guide middle schoolers through this difficult time.

Reflection

1. Review the characteristics from this chapter and compare it against the students on your class roster whom you know are identified as gifted. Are there any you find surprising on the list? Are there any students you are surprised are not included?

References

Apter, T. (2009, January 19). Teens and parents in conflict. Blog post. Psychology Today. Retrieved from www.psychologytoday.com/us/blog/domestic-intelligence/200901/teens-and-parents-in-conflict

Baldwin, L., Omdal, S. N., & Pereles, D. (2015). Beyond stereotypes: Understanding, recognizing, and working with twice-exceptional learners. *Teaching Exceptional Children*, *47*(4), 216–225. https://doi.org/10.1177/0040059915569361

Besnoy, K. D., Jolly, J. L., & Manning, S. (2011). Academic underachievement of gifted students. In J. A. Castellano & A. D. Frazier (Eds.), *Special populations in gifted education: Understanding our most able students from diverse backgrounds* (pp. 401–415). Prufrock Press Inc.

Bishop, J. (2021, March 1). Overexcitabilities: Not everyone is excited about them. Blog post. National Association for Gifted Children. Retrieved from www.nagc.org/blog/overexcitabilities-not-everyone-excited-about-them

Castellano, J. A., & Frazier, A. D. (Eds.). (2011). *Special populations in gifted education: Understanding our most able students from diverse backgrounds*. Prufrock Press Inc.

Clark, B. (2002). *Growing up gifted* (6th ed.). Merrill Prentice Hall.

Lind, S. (2011, September 14). Overexcitability and the gifted. SENG. Retrieved from www.sengifted.org/post/overexcitability-and-the-gifted

National Association for Gifted Children. (n.d.). Identifying gifted children from diverse populations. Retrieved September 5, 2022, from www.nagc.org/resources-publications/resources/timely-topics/ensuring-diverse-learner-participation-gifted-0

National Association for Gifted Children. (2008). The role of assessments in the identification of gifted students. Position Statement. Retrieved from nagc.org/sites/default/files/Position%20Statement/Assessment%20 Position%20Statement.pdf

National Association for Gifted Children. (2019). A definition of giftedness that guides best practice. Position Statement. Retrieved from www. nagc.org/sites/default/files/Position%20Statement/Definition%20 of%20Giftedness%20%282019%29.pdf

Peters, S. J., & Engerrand, K. G. (2016). Equity and excellence: Proactive efforts in the identification of underrepresented students for gifted and talented services. *Gifted Child Quarterly*, *60*(3), 159–171. https://doi. org/10.1177/0016986216643165

Peters, S. J., Gentry, M., Whiting, G. W., & McBee, M. T. (2019). Who gets served in gifted education? Demographic representation and a call for action. *Gifted Child Quarterly*, *63*(4), 273–287. https://doi.org/ 10.1177/0016986219833738

Piitro, J. (2004). *Understanding creativity*. Great Potential Press, Inc.

Raimi, S. (Director). (2004, June 25). *Spider-Man 2*. Sony Pictures Releasing.

Rinn, A. N., Mun, R. U., & Hodges, J. (2020). *2018–2019 State of the states in gifted education*. Available at www.nagc.org/2018-2019-state-sta tes-gifted-education

Silverman, L. K. (1997). The construct of asynchronous development. *Peabody Journal of Education*, *72*(3/4), 36–58.

Sousa, D. A. (2009). *How the gifted brain learns* (2nd ed.). Corwin.

The dress. (2022). In Wikipedia. Retrieved from https://en.wikipedia.org/w/ index.php?title=The_dress&oldid=1103779828

Webb, J. T. (Ed.). (2016). *Misdiagnosis and dual diagnoses of gifted children and adults: ADHD, bipolar, OCD, Asperger's, depression, and other disorders* (2nd ed.). Great Potential Press, Inc.

Winebrenner, S., & Brulles, D. (2018). *Teaching gifted kids in today's class-room* (4th ed.). Free Spirit Publishing.

Looking in the Mirror and Liking Who You See

Middle school is a confusing time.

Not only are adolescents dealing with significant physical changes, but they are caught in this weird limbo between childhood and adulthood. Former passions become "uncool," and there is an entirely new set of social expectations. There are so many added pressures that were not present before, and social media adds a whole other dimension. What makes this even more difficult is that no matter how hard we, as adults, try to relate, the world middle schoolers face today is far different than anything previous generations experienced.

Being gifted adds another layer to this experience. On top of needing instruction that supports their academic needs, many gifted students struggle to find friends and peers to whom they can relate (Delisle & Galbraith, 2002). While this is difficult at any time, in middle school, social interactions and relationships often can take precedence. Many gifted adolescents are placed in a situation where their academic needs are in conflict with their social needs (Guthrie, 2020). This is like the 2001 episode of *The Simpsons*, where the father of the family, Homer, learns the cause of his lack of intelligence. After a medical procedure greatly improves his IQ, he discovers the challenges of being smart. While he uses his intellect to make improvements in the world around him, he subsequently loses all his friends. At the end of the episode, he decides to reverse the procedure to regain his happiness, losing everything he gained, even the newfound relationship he developed with his gifted daughter (Anderson, 2001).

For gifted students, the push and pull between being themselves and fitting in is extremely complicated, and gifted middle school students are

DOI: 10.4324/9781003332015-3

particularly vulnerable to underachievement (Besnoy et al., 2011). This time is incredibly important, however, as it is during these years that adolescents begin defining who they will be.

Who Am I?

Humanity's search for self-discovery is a foundational journey we take. Psychologist Erik Erikson identified Eight Stages of Development in this process, with each stage associated with major milestones an individual goes through during their life. The adolescent phase, which lasts from approximately 12 to 18, is when young people are considering their identities, goals, and their place within the world (Erikson, 1968). Identity is a driving force that guides how a person understands themselves and can have a profound impact on their future.

As gifted individuals enter middle school, the change in structure can influence the ways in which they see themselves. For many, they have experienced success and support in elementary school, and leaving this environment can be jarring. The structure, relationships with teachers, and the focus of the students all change. In many ways, the sense of understanding of themselves they have entering middle school can be shattered as the environmental expectations are completely different (Besnoy et al., 2011). By losing this foundation, gifted middle school students not only lose their confidence, but also must consider how their identity fits within this new atmosphere.

This can be detrimental in many ways, but one of the most tangible ways teachers and parents can see this manifest is through academic underperformance. As students enter adolescence, their peer relationships take priority. Their understanding of success (achieving and maintaining good grades) changes from elementary to middle school, and gifted students can begin to hide their abilities to fit in (Besnoy et al., 2011). Another contributing factor to this is the challenge that comes with middle school, both the organizational components and the rigor of the work, which can cause students to doubt themselves at a time when most are figuring out who they are (Besnoy et al., 2011).

Culture Development

Whenever I have seen inspiring stories about educators who make a difference in their classrooms or with their students, one of the constant themes is the culture those teachers create. While the methods they use might be different, they create an environment where students are comfortable, take risks, and are able to grow. Even in popular culture this trend is present. In many education movies, from *Freedom Writers* to *Dead Poets Society* to *Stand and Deliver*, to reach their students, the teacher must first create a classroom culture that allows this happen.

For example, my favorite education movie is *X-Men: First Class*. While that might seem like an odd choice, being a superhero movie and all, at the core, it represents everything that being an educator of gifted students is about. Acting as a prequel to the X-Men movies where a portion of the population are born with genetic mutations that grant them incredible abilities, the film follows Charles Xavier shortly after leaving graduate school. Charles is a mutant and has witnessed the fear and ostracism others like him have experienced, resulting in most living in hiding. While the film has its goal – for the X-Men to save the world, a large portion of it is devoted to Charles working with his first class of students, helping them to harness their gifts. To do this, though, he must create a culture where they not only understand how special each of them is, but are able to celebrate one another. Each student had to hide who they were for so long, yet Xavier created an atmosphere where they could take risks and learn without fear of judgment. From accommodating somebody who shoots lasers by letting him practice in a fallout shelter to helping his friend harness positive emotions to achieve more than he thought possible, Xavier built them up (Vaughn, 2011). While there isn't a one-size-fits-all solution that will work for every child or classroom, one of the most valuable things a middle school teacher can do is to establish a positive, supporting culture.

While there are many ways culture can be defined, the *Harvard Business Review* defines it "as the ways people in the organization behave and the attitudes and beliefs that inform those behaviors (i.e., 'the way we do things around here') — including formal, stated norms as well as implicit ways people work and interact" (Yohn, 2021, para. 4). Each day students come into a classroom, adjusting their behaviors to fit the norms and expectations of the teacher. Think about discussions you've had or overheard between teachers talking about an individual student. A phrase like, "I've never seen that student act that way in my class," is one I have heard quite often. In a typical school day, a middle school student is adjusting their behavior up to seven times to meet the explicit and hidden expectations of the teacher and the other students. In my experience of conducting teacher observations, the impact that classroom culture can have on students is significant as they adjust not just their behavior, but their attitudes as well.

It is also important to note that while classroom management is an important element of culture, it is just one component. Students need expectations of how they navigate a situation, as well as an understanding of how their behaviors impact others. A well-managed classroom allows students to access curriculum and learn in a safe environment. This should be used as a platform to develop culture, but it is not all that defines it.

While every class is different, I've found four core cultural elements that contribute to an environment which encourages gifted students to be themselves as they develop their identities: acceptance, respect, support, and understanding.

Acceptance

One of the most profound ways to support gifted middle school students as they search for their identities is to create a culture of acceptance, where any student can come to the class free of judgment. While acceptance is important for any age group, at middle school this becomes key, as social dynamics play a more significant role.

As teachers, one of the things we ask our students to do is take risks in the classroom. We ask them to volunteer more in class, give presentations, and take leadership roles. These are all critical skills we need to develop, but we need to ensure that the classroom culture supports these risks. Gifted students tend to be incredibly observant and perceptive; they are paying attention to everything happening in a classroom and processing the best course of action. The way that a teacher or the class responds in any situation are all data that inform whether what they say or do will be accepted.

It is also important to understand that, during adolescence, gifted students are in a place of self-discovery, considering the different paths they might take (Wood & Szymanski, 2020). One of the concepts associated with this is the idea of "possible selves," which addresses the ways in which individuals view and imagine their future (Markus & Nurius, 1986). Like looking into the multiverse, our gifted students see a variety of potential paths they can take, and adolescence is the time in which they begin to explore these options. Our classrooms become one of the arenas in which they begin this exploration, and they need to know they can be themselves without judgment.

Respect

When students and teachers respect one another, there is a freedom in the way ideas are shared, and students are more willing to take academic and social risks, as they know that their perspectives are valued. Thinking of the traits of gifted students, they tend to be divergent thinkers, thinking outside the box or approaching problems and questions from unique angles (Clark, 2002). This is one of those traits that many teachers I have talked to love about their gifted students, but, at middle school, divergence in thinking is counterproductive. Middle school is often characterized by a need to fit in and going against the status quo can not only make a student stand out but also draw overt negative attention.

Changing an entire school culture takes time, dedication, and a focused effort from teachers and administrators, but changes within a classroom can start immediately. Establishing an understanding that different perspectives and ideas will be respected, even if there is disagreement, is a powerful thing.

This culture of respect is one of the first things I try to establish in my class. I have always taught English and history, and most of my lessons are taught through discussion, allowing students to generate their own ideas and thoughts about the content. Because there is so much flexibility in the way students can interpret the material, there are naturally conflicting ideas. However, these disagreements are valuable to help students develop critical thinking, learn how to defend their perspectives, and be open to different ideas.

I once had a gifted student who had very strong views, and their perspectives ran very contrary to those of the rest of the class. Every time we had a discussion, they would have differing opinions from their peers and even had a separate folder filled with evidence to argue their points. This naturally created some tension, as the other students, who were all also gifted, had very strong opinions on the other side.

To make sure the culture of the class did not dissolve and that there was respect between these different perspectives, I modeled for my students what respectful discourse looked like. I made a point of highlighting positive aspects of the two different perspectives when they came up in discussion. By showing the students the value of what each side had to offer in the natural flow of conversation, it demonstrated that there was worth on each side. I would then follow up the positive acknowledgment with a question to allow alternative perspectives to come through. By setting it up in this way, the discussions became focused on the ideas instead of the students trying to prove each other wrong. Eventually, just through the natural development of our class, students were acknowledging and discussing points that were the opposite of what they believed. While they still held on to their core beliefs, they were able to understand alternative perspectives, and this only comes from a culture of respect.

This also empowers students to understand that their beliefs have value. Since many gifted students have a strong sense of justice (Clark, 2002), understanding how to stand up for what they believe in allows those elements of their identity to continue developing. At a time when standing out is the last thing most students want to do, we can create a classroom environment that embraces this idea.

Support

One of the biggest myths of gifted education is that gifted students don't need support and they'll just figure it out (National Association for Gifted Children, n.d.). Gifted students have advanced abilities and so much potential, but that does not mean they will be successful without help and support. Just like any student, gifted students need the guidance of their teachers, but what I think is more important, is that they know this need is alright. We will discuss perfectionism specifically in Chapter 3, but this is an important element to address in culture building.

I have seen the same scenario play out countless times in my classroom, where I check in with students, and they tell me everything is going great; however, the message I hear from home is the opposite. Parents have shared that their child will stay up late to make sure an assignment is perfect or comb through myriad resources hoping to find an answer to a question they might have. For a question I could answer quickly, they have sacrificed their time and energy, all to avoid asking for help.

While there is no single cause for this, middle school can be the first academic challenge gifted students face (Besnoy et al., 2011). As a result, they have not previously had to advocate for their needs, and that can make the entire process feel overwhelming and defeating. Students need to know that asking for help is not a weakness, and, as a classroom, everybody supports each other.

Understanding

One of the most human things I can think of is our capacity to make mistakes. Just when we think we have it all figured out, we find some way to stumble. It does not matter how old you are; if you are human, you are going to make errors, and adolescence is a prime time for this.

Throughout my time teaching gifted middle schoolers, I have seen students make a lot of mistakes, including but not limited to:

- forgetting to do homework, turn in homework, or come to class
- procrastinating on a major project
- not waking up and missing school
- using a disrespectful tone in an email
- lying
- breaking a laptop
- using a book to block a projector and burning a hole in said book
- getting so overwhelmed by the sheer amount of work and responsibilities they kicked a hole in a wall.

If you did not do this already, please look at the list and think about how you would respond in each of those situations. While there is no perfect answer, there is a common need throughout each of those mistakes: a need for understanding.

Adolescence is a difficult time, as students are caught in this limbo between being adults and being kids. There are so many pressures on students this age when their entire world has changed. Even though they are still kids, there is often this expectation that they are little adults. For gifted students, this is even more of a challenge with asynchronous development, as their intellect often is working at a profound level above their age, yet they respond to hardships the same way as their age-level peers or younger (Silverman, 1997). It is critical, that when our students make a mistake, they know we will be understanding.

Having a student kick a hole in a wall is one of those teacher moments I will never forget. It was near the end of the school year, and I was teaching in a self-contained middle school gifted program. For this program, I taught humanities and worked alongside a science teacher. While we each had our own separate classes, there was a shared space between our two rooms that we could use for collaboration, and the students often moved seamlessly between our two classes during work time.

The science teacher and I were doing a very large integrated project with the entire program that addressed multiple content areas. I could sense the feeling of stress as the project deadline drew closer, and one of the students received feedback on the science portion of their assignment. I was in my room working with some students when I heard a loud *thud* from the shared room. The student who received science feedback came back to my class, laid their head down, and began crying. Before I could check on the student, my teaching partner came to get me, and she told me the student had kicked a hole in the wall of our shared room.

We called the student aside to ask what happened. Between sobs, they explained they thought they were told they had to add something new to the project. They were so overwhelmed by everything going on in their life they kicked the wall in frustration. They didn't expect their foot to go through the wall, and then they apologized profusely.

After I heard the story, the only way I could react was to laugh.

When the student saw me laugh their initial reaction was surprise, and then they started to cry-laugh. After a moment of laughter, we all composed ourselves, and talked about what happened, how overwhelmed the student was, and how we could help them. This was a critical moment for this student, and the way we reacted had the potential to be contentious or to help them grow. Obviously, there were consequences, but I spoke with my principal who knew middle school students incredibly well, and we worked together with the student and family to find a solution. In a moment that could have destroyed the relationship with that student, we strengthened it. They did not need us to add another layer of stress on their life, but rather, needed us to be there for them.

When talking about understanding as a cultural component, I've had teachers express concerns about being "too soft" or "too lenient," and I want to address some of those concerns.

1. *What if they take advantage of it?* This concern comes from the thought that if we show grace to a student, they will abuse it and repeat the same behavior. For example, if a project is incomplete by the due date, the concern is that giving an extension will mean extensions will be asked for every project. This thinking, while it might be based on experience, presents a distinct lack of trust between teacher and student. Every situation is different, and we need to acknowledge and try to understand the factors that are leading to a behavior. Granting an extension on a project by itself does not mean that the student will turn in every assignment late, just like not yelling at the student for kicking the wall does not mean they are going to continue to kick holes in walls.

    Part of understanding is listening to the factors that contribute to an outcome and working together to address the behavior. If a student is not done with a project, the next question should be "Why?" By understanding the components that led to that moment, we can then work together to find solutions and prevent that from happening again. Did the student not plan time appropriately throughout the project? Did the student get lost in the content because they were so interested, they forgot actually to do the project? Does the student have to take care of younger siblings while the parents work? Does the student not have internet access or a computer at home? Each of these reasons requires a different type of support, but we can only provide that support if we understand what the student is experiencing.

2. *I need to prepare them for high school/the real world.* This is a concern that is coming from a good place, but, in execution, it is often just punishing students for skills they might not have developed. Many gifted students have not had to work hard to achieve good grades in their classes. At the beginning of each school year, I've asked my

27

self-contained gifted classes to share how many of them have waited until the last minute to complete a big project and still gotten an A. Almost every student raises their hand. What this means is that when gifted students get to middle school, they have not learned how to budget or manage their time.

In addition, one component of asynchronous development is a lack of judgment (Webb, 2016). This also coincides biologically, as the prefrontal cortex, which addresses planning and judgment, develops more slowly than the parts of the brain which address academic areas (Webb, 2016). While accountability is incredibly important, by punishing students who have never learned to manage their time, we are not actually preparing them. How to break down a large project, use a planner, and study effectively are skills that students need to be taught. Awarding zeros for missing assignments might feel like teaching a lesson, but without the actual support, it is just punitive.

One of the ways I have done this in my classes is to frontload an experience of time management in a small project at the beginning of the year. To do this, I establish a working timeline for the class and let them know I am a resource if they need support. During the project, I check in with students, but I let them drive the role I play. Typically, most are very independent during this process, but, as the due date gets closer, I can feel the stress start to build. This is an expected part of the experience, and, as a class, we debrief on the way the project is developing, discuss errors they made in planning, and then plan the next steps for how to complete the project. Usually, the due date is adjusted with their new understanding, but this was all an intended component from the beginning. With subsequent projects, the students now understand better how to manage their time and are more receptive to my guidance. In addition, in showing them understanding during this initial project, we develop a strong trust. The students are still held accountable, but I have worked with them on how to achieve what is expected. In doing this, rather than just punishing them, the students are more prepared for high school and the future.

3. *It's not fair to the rest of the class if I make an exception for just one student.* This is another consideration that I understand, but, just like the first two, context is everything. Each situation should be evaluated

on its own. The other point that needs to be understood, is that our students have lives outside of our classes. They will experience things, both good and bad, that take priority over our assignments and projects, and we need to be understanding. One of the ways to lessen the impact of individual exceptions is to establish early that you want students to communicate with you if they have a need. Establishing this up front helps students to know you care and helps develop self-advocacy skills. This is the same policy every graduate school class I have ever taught or taken uses, and it's a valuable one for students to learn.

One other point I think is important to address with this concern is that any exception or adjustment you make for one student can apply to the rest of the class. While I do not make a habit of changing due dates for every student, it is important to get a pulse of how your class is feeling, especially after a student voices a concern. If one student identifies that they are overwhelmed with the amount they need to do, there is a likelihood that they are not alone. Understanding how each of your classes is feeling empowers you to be responsive and build your relationship with your students, while also emphasizing the support element of culture building.

Developing Classroom Culture

Culture development is a topic that many have spoken about. From businesses to classrooms to families, there is an ongoing discussion about how we develop this element that can make such a difference. Entire books could be written about this topic, but my goal is to give you three strategies for developing your classroom culture to create an environment that will support gifted middle school students in establishing their identity.

First, it is important to be direct regarding those cultural elements on which you want your class to focus. Often, we assume that students understand or know our expectations, but they sometimes just need to be told. In addition, for gifted students, providing explanation and the reasoning behind an expectation is incredibly valuable, as it helps frame what you are wanting. At the beginning of the school year, when classroom norms are being addressed, this is a great time to establish those cultural elements you want the class to embody. For example, in my history class, I explain to students that knowing the facts is important, but I am more interested in their ideas, questions, and our class discussions. I then discuss the four cultural elements, providing examples of what this looks like from me and how it can look from the class. By frontloading this discussion, it helps ensure that the students know from the first day of class how they fit into the classroom.

It is also important to note that this direct acknowledgment of classroom culture does not just happen on the first day of school but is consistently addressed throughout the school year. For example, when I know that a topic in history will result in divided opinions, I re-establish my cultural expectations before the lesson even begins.

A second way to establish a culture of identity development is to give positive reinforcement when students demonstrate what we are expecting. I make a habit of having one-on-one conversations with students to informally tell them the things that they do well. This can be content or behavior based, but I also try to incorporate those cultural elements as well. These conversations can go a long way in not just developing culture, but also the relationship with that student. Gifted students value authenticity (Cross, 2021), and in providing direct and specific positive feedback, we show them that we see them as an individual, thus reinforcing those elements of identity development. In addition, during these one-on-ones, I will ask students if they are OK with me highlighting similar behaviors for the whole class. In asking for their permission, we help to reinforce their developing independence and control of their lives. While most students I've asked have been fine with me addressing the whole class, for those who are not comfortable, this is incredibly powerful; they have a voice that is respected.

A third way to establish this culture is to model it as a teacher. Of all the strategies, this is the most important. If we want our class to embody certain values, we need to live by those as well. As we have already mentioned, gifted students tend to be incredibly observant, paying attention to everything happening in the classroom. In addition, they tend to have a strong sense of justice, and take great issue with hypocrisy (Clark, 2002). It takes time to build trust, but that trust can be lost very quickly. If we do not embody what we ask of our students, not only will we not get the culture we want, but it will create friction and conflict with the class.

When I Call Your Name

"Bueller? Bueller? Bueller?" (Hughes, 1986).

This quotation from the 1986 film *Ferris Bueller's Day Off* captures the way most people think of classroom attendance: for a portion of the class period, everyone waits in silence while the teacher calls out names, and the student who was called declares they are present. Day in and day out it is the same process, and in many classes, when the teacher gets to know the students, they will stop calling the names altogether. This exchange is how most classes are started. While important, it is also incredibly boring, but it does not have to be. We have a time during our class period where each student is given an opportunity to address the entire class without interruption, and by changing up how we take attendance, we can learn more about our students and help them develop their understanding of who they are.

In my class, they've come to be known as "fun attendances," where, instead of saying "here," I have students answer a prescribed question. Sometimes the students are given two options and sometimes the question is open-ended, but the attendance always starts with the phrase, "When I call your name... ." At the core, these are essentially ice breakers that engage the class and help them get to know their peers, but in a bigger sense, they shift the tone and culture of the classroom. This silly time becomes something that the students look forward to, and if I do not start the class with a "fun attendance," they feel like they have had something taken away. For example, I was teaching a class of high school juniors, and they seemed apathetic to my attendance questions. I decided not to ask a silly question to save time, and, as I was working through the class list, one of the students interrupted me, and asked, "Where is our fun attendance?" The rest of the class echoed their question, and, when I told them I thought they did not like these fun questions, they assured me that they did. I then restarted attendance, even though I already had it marked.

While asking 30 students to answer a question every day takes up more time than the traditional method, the laughter and excitement amongst the students makes it worthwhile. For gifted students, this also provides an opportunity for "intellectual" debate, where they are providing their own logic in answering a question, even if it is a simple "Would You Rather" prompt. Asking a room of 12–13-year-old gifted students whether they would want to read minds or turn invisible can lead to some heated discussion and justification. More importantly, though, these attendances provide a safe, non-threatening platform to build experience in expressing opinions without fear of judgment, which, in middle school, can be a challenge.

These attendances have been one of the easiest ways that I have found to develop culture in my classroom, and I have had many parents tell me that their children will come home and ask the attendance question to their family. The first five minutes of class can be filled with laughter as students weigh the merits of which type of pasta would make the best hair, but it also makes them more comfortable and open for the class period.

I've also been able to learn a lot about my students through these attendances, and I could spend a great deal of time discussing all the questions I have asked my classes throughout the years. The Appendix is a categorical list that you can use to get started asking "fun attendances" in your classroom. As you use more of these prompts, you'll get a feel for what your class likes, and you can add your own. It is also important to note that these attendances do take up more class time, so you'll need to plan accordingly. To start, it might be best to try one dynamic attendance a week, as your class gets more comfortable with answering the questions and you understand the impact this has on your lesson plan for the day.

While asking silly questions can be a lot of fun, I also use attendance to help provide meaningful self-reflection for the students. The three questions I want to highlight require students to show a great deal of vulnerability, and it is important that you do not lead with these questions. Students should feel comfortable in your class, and you need to feel confident in the culture you have created. In addition, while the other questions I ask will be sprung on the students on the day, with these three questions, I give the students a day in advance to think about their response.

When I Call Your Name, Please Tell Me Something You Like about Your Neighbor

Middle school is a time when adolescents feel judged by the world, and hearing something positive from their peers can make a world of difference. I have never felt more touched as a teacher than watching a class of middle schoolers all say the great things they see their peers do.

This is an attendance that takes some preparation work ahead of time, as expectations need to be clearly stated. When I introduce this prompt, I always begin with a restatement of our cultural norms, and the importance of supporting our peers. In addition, I also make sure to establish that there will be no sarcasm, backhanded compliments, or veiled criticism. With those norms established, I have never had an issue, but I have made sure to pull certain students aside before attendance to make sure that they fully understand what is expected.

When I Call Your Name, Please Tell Me a Dream You Have

This attendance question requires students to show an incredible amount of vulnerability, but it can also lead to the greatest insight into who they are and what motivates them. In classes where I feel like I know each of the students incredibly well, I get surprised by a dream they have. Through asking this question, it also helps in their formation of their identity. As part of Erikson's stages of adolescent identity development, students try to establish their goals for the next phase of their lives (Erikson, 1968), and this also connects to the idea of "possible selves" discussed earlier (Markus & Nurius, 1986). Asking this question can help students begin to frame their goals and verbalize what they want to do. Understanding their dreams and aspirations then allows me to provide support and guidance for them, which, in turn, helps to develop that sense of identity.

This attendance also highlights an important aspect of dynamic attendance questions: you should participate as well.

In asking our students to be vulnerable we need to demonstrate that same vulnerability. We want them to trust us, so in turn, we need to trust them. When I ask a question that requires openness like this, I will typically be the first to respond to demonstrate the trust I have in them.

When I Call Your Name, Please Tell Me Something You Like about Yourself

Of all the attendances I have done, sadly, this is the one that middle school students struggle with the most. While some of that comes from a place of not wanting to be arrogant, for many, there is a vulnerability in sharing something so personal. In addition, many gifted adolescents have not struggled through elementary school, but with the shifting norms and expectations of middle school, their self-confidence can be shaken (Besnoy et al., 2011). Asking students not to listen to the negative self-talk and see all the great things about who they are can be difficult.

While in most of my attendances I let students "pass" if they do not have an answer, this is one in which I strongly encourage every student to participate. I establish ahead of time that they all have countless things they should be proud of, and I want them to highlight just one, no matter how big or small. Like the "something you like about your neighbor" prompt, I also establish that I do not want students to be self-deprecating in their responses. Even if the response is superficial or small, I want them to identify something they like about themselves.

Despite these norms, I still have students struggle with this question. I will usually ask them if they need more time to think of a response, but sometimes they still struggle. When this happens, usually I will highlight something great I see in them, trying to give them a direction in which to take their response. When I've had these situations happen where a student is hesitant to share, I have also seen something magical happen: unprompted, their peers will start celebrating the student. Students who can't think of a positive thing to say about themselves have had half the class start sharing how special they are.

Middle school can be a time when adolescents feel like they are all alone, but moments like this demonstrate the power of a positive classroom culture in feeling connected.

Summary

Adolescence is crucial time for students as it begins their journey of self-discovery and identity development. At this age, students are starting to consider what their goals are and how they want to fit into the world; however, middle school also represents a stark shift in the structures and norms that students once knew and understood. As a result, this time is confusing, challenging, and stressful. As teachers, one of the ways that we can support this is through establishing a classroom culture of acceptance, respect, support, and understanding. By creating this environment, students can take social and academic risks in that ultimate quest of self-discovery.

Reflection

The reflection for this section has two components: personal self-reflection and classroom practice reflection. The personal self-reflection prompts align with the ideas of identity development our gifted middle school students are experiencing. While Erikson identifies identity development as an adolescent stage, I personally feel this is a question we are always answering. The classroom practice reflection question asks you to consider ways in which you can apply the lessons from this chapter in your own teaching.

Self-Reflection

1. What is your "why" for being a teacher? What is your big picture goal as you start each lesson?
2. What is something you like about yourself?

Classroom Practice Reflection

1. Assess your classroom culture. Are there elements you need to adjust to create an environment that is more conducive to student identity development?

References

Anderson, M. (Director). (2001, January 7). HOMR (No. 257) [TV series episode]. In *The Simpsons*. Fox.

Besnoy, K. D., Jolly, J. L., & Manning, S. (2011). Academic underachievement of gifted students. In J. A. Castellano & A. D. Frazier (Eds.), *Special populations in gifted education: Understanding our most able students from diverse backgrounds* (pp. 401–415). Prufrock Press Inc.

Clark, B. (2002). *Growing up gifted* (6th ed.). Merrill Prentice Hall.

Cross, T. L. (2021). Social and emotional development: The role of authenticity in the psychosocial development of students with gifts and talents. *Gifted Child Today*, *44*(2), 111–114. https://doi.org/10.1177/10762 17520988777

Delisle, J., & Galbraith, J. (2002). *When gifted kids don't have all the answers*. Free Spirit Publishing.

Erikson, E. H. (1968). *Identity: Youth and crisis*. W. W. Norton & Company Inc.

Guthrie, K. H. (2020). The weight of expectations: A thematic narrative of gifted adolescent girls' reflections of being gifted. *Roeper Review*, *42*(1), 25–37. https://doi.org/10.1080/02783193.2019.1690080

Hughes, J. (Director). (1986). *Ferris Bueller's Day Off* [Film]. Paramount Pictures.

Markus, H., & Nurius, P. (1986). Possible selves. *American Psychologist*, *41*(9), 954–969. https://doi.org/10.1037/0003-066X.41.9.954

National Association for Gifted Children. (n.d.). Myths about gifted students. Retrieved April 18, 2021, from www.nagc.org/myths-about-gifted-students

Silverman, L. K. (1997). The construct of asynchronous development. *Peabody Journal of Education*, *72*(3/4), 36–58.

Vaughn, M. (Director). (2011). *X-Men: First Class* [Film]. 20th Century Fox.

Webb, J. T. (Ed.). (2016). *Misdiagnosis and dual diagnoses of gifted children and adults: ADHD, bipolar, OCD, Asperger's, depression, and other disorders* (2nd ed.). Great Potential Press, Inc.

Wood, S. M., & Szymanski, A. (2020). "The me I want you to see": The use of video game avatars to explore identity in gifted adolescents. *Gifted Child Today*, *43*(2), 124–134. https://doi.org/10.1177/10762 17519898217

Yohn, D. L. (2021, February 8). Company culture is everyone's responsibility. *Harvard Business Review*. Retrieved from https://hbr.org/2021/02/company-culture-is-everyones-responsibility

A Mantra Not
Worth Living By

In the 2006 film *Talladega Nights: The Ballad of Ricky Bobby*, the title character has a saying: "If you ain't first, you're last" (McKay, 2006). This phrase becomes a guiding principle for Will Ferrell's character who, to regain his place as the top NASCAR (stock car racing) driver, alienates his friends, all in the pursuit of glory. When Ricky Bobby eventually confronts his father about this saying, his father highlights the ridiculous nature of this mantra, identifying that there are a lot of other places than first (McKay, 2006). While this scene is played for laughs in a film filled with over-the-top moments, there is a harsh reality we need to understand: whether intentional or not, this is a motto by which many of our gifted students live.

Perfectionism

The *Merriam-Webster Dictionary* defines perfectionism as "a disposition to regard anything short of perfection as unacceptable" (Merriam-Webster, n.d.). The key word that we need to consider with this definition is "unacceptable." While it is valuable to have high standards and work hard, the reality is that "perfect" is an impossible goal. There is always something that can be improved, always a component to adjust, let alone considerations of the unique perspectives and interests of different audiences. Setting the bar at perfection only creates an outcome of disappointment (Delisle & Galbraith, 2002).

For gifted students this is especially concerning, as the NAGC notes that roughly 20% of gifted children experience perfectionism in a way that

DOI: 10.4324/9781003332015-4

creates problems (National Association for Gifted Children, n.d.). With nearly one in five of our gifted population having perfectionism impact them in such a dynamic way, it is important that we understand this problem and what it can look like.

There is no one single explanation for how these behaviors appear, but there are some common ways in which the negative aspects of perfectionism can manifest in gifted students. The first and most obvious is that students will dedicate excessive amounts of time to assignments to ensure that they are perfect (Winebrenner & Brulles, 2018). This drive might seem positive at first, but the reality is that sustaining that level of rigor for an extended period is not possible. This is especially true when we consider the amount that is being asked of middle school students.

If we just narrow homework down to core academic areas (English, math, science, and history), that is potentially four different subjects a student might have to complete homework on any given night. If a student, attempting to reach lofty goals of perfection, adds half an hour to each of those four assignments, that is an additional two hours of work on top of whatever was being asked. From my experience, though, this estimate is low, and when other classes are added to that equation, it only becomes more unreasonable. Because there are a finite number of hours in the day, if students are not able to complete their work to perfection before bedtime, I've had many parents tell me that their child stays up late to finish. They are withdrawing hours from their sleep, which, in turn, has an even bigger impact, as this is now impacting their sleep and ability to be rested for the next day.

Another negative behavior that can manifest with perfectionism is devastation over anything short of the perceived goal. I have a very clear memory of this from early in my career teaching gifted middle schoolers. The class had just finished taking a test on Ray Bradbury's novel *Fahrenheit 451*, and the average on the test was low. As a result, I let the class perform test corrections to earn back some of the missing points. When I returned the tests, one student saw that they did not earn an A even after the corrections and let out a sound that can only be described as a howl. They were distraught and near inconsolable over the grade, even after I assured them this one grade would not prevent them from still earning an A in my class.

These reactions do make sense, however, especially when we consider asynchronous development. These students are reasoning and thinking in profound ways, some even at the college level, but emotionally, many of them are still kids (Silverman, 1997). For some gifted students, this is combined with never having experienced a result that was less than perfect. In an instant, their understanding of success and their self-worth can come crashing down.

This can be seen in students refusing to even begin assignments for fear that, since they cannot do it perfectly, they should not even start (Winebrenner & Brulles, 2018). This behavior seems counterintuitive, as, to avoid failing, the student turns in nothing. While the result is still failure, the student can avoid negative feedback. In essence, since they feel like they are already going to fail, they might as well fail on their own terms.

I had a student once who exhibited a similar behavior, but took it a step farther. I once met with a family whose child was failing my class, yet not showing any signs that they did not understand the content. The parents explained how confused they were by the grade, as they saw their child working every night. When we asked the student about it, they explained that they were afraid they would not do well, so they chose not to turn in the work they completed. Weeks of work sat in their Google Drive, unseen by anybody.

These aren't the only behaviors gifted students exhibit with perfectionism, but I feel they highlight the negative impact this perspective can have. Middle school is challenging enough as it is, and having students feeling like they need to meet an unattainable goal is just making this time more difficult.

Maybe I'm the Problem

In season 4 of NBC's *The Office*, one of the employees of the office has a heart attack. The boss, Michael Scott, attempts to help lower the stress of his employees by leading a meditation session, only to find out that *he* is the source of stress for most of his staff. In a documentary-like address to the camera, Michael explains, "You never expect that you're the killer; it's a great twist" (Blitz, 2009). While I don't think any teachers expect to perpetuate perfectionistic tendencies in their students, the reality is that there are subtle things we do that can send home the message that anything less than perfect is unacceptable.

This influence can start early, well before gifted students join our middle school classes. During these early years, work can come very easily for gifted students, and, often, they are told how smart they are. While this is not bad in and of itself, it does create a concerning precedent, where gifted students begin to associate their worth with doing well. If the only feedback gifted students receive is not directed at the task itself (you did well), but rather the student (you are smart), then it is wrapping their entire academic identity around the quality of the work they submit.

This becomes increasingly concerning as gifted students get older. As the content naturally becomes more complex, it can be harder for gifted students to maintain this sense of perfection (Besnoy et al., 2011). In addition, by not experiencing challenge or failure in the same way at a younger age, gifted students do not develop the coping skills necessary to handle falling short of their own expectations. If the first time a student experiences a disappointment like that is in middle school, then it only makes sense that the student reaction is more extreme.

While the foundation of perfectionism can be established in the earlier grades, the ways teachers approach talking about grades and student work in middle school can still create a warped sense of identity. For example, the feedback we provide students on their work can have an incredible impact. Phrases like "you can do better" or "I expected more" might seem positive and encouraging, but the reality is that this sort of feedback puts an unnecessary pressure on gifted students (Winebrenner & Brulles, 2018).

A for Effort

Although there is no easy fix for perfectionism, there are things that we can do as teachers to help support our gifted middle schoolers. We must be conscientious with the feedback we provide and place the emphasis on the effort and work students contributed rather than the product. It is very easy to be results motivated, but this small adjustment in the language used can have a massive impact.

This shift in the way feedback is provided is something I have become very aware of as a parent. As I write this, my daughter is three years old, and, while my wife and I want nothing more than to tell our daughter how amazing and wonderful she is, we make a concerted effort to celebrate the work she puts into any task. We still tell her how great she is, but we also emphasize something specific she did well or a specific problem she overcame. This shift in feedback can even be found in the television she watches. In the 2019 reboot of the TV series *Blue's Clues*, *Blue's Clues & You!*, an addition was made to the classic goodbye song, adding a reference to working hard in addition to being smart (Burns & Horhager, 2019). This simple change acknowledges that hard work does not detract from somebody being smart. We can all use this lesson from *Blue's Clues & You!* to help frame our feedback.

Ongoing feedback to students while they are working on assignments or projects is a strategy for emphasizing hard work. This serves two purposes in supporting perfectionistic students. First, by providing feedback while students are working on a project, it allows for more natural comments regarding the effort being placed. For example, when I taught the self-contained gifted middle school class, I utilized mostly project-based assignments. Many times, students would create movies, websites, or other multimedia projects to demonstrate their learning. While they had ongoing work time, I would cycle from student to student, providing feedback and support. Since I could see them in the process of creation, I was able to provide immediate feedback, often identifying the moments of struggle, which allowed us to not only work through challenges, but also celebrate the victories that came. This also supports an existing strategy of utilizing goal setting, where they identify smaller goals to reach their bigger ones (Winebrenner & Brulles, 2018). By framing for students what they need to complete, it makes tasks that seem insurmountable achievable. Through these smaller tasks, success and support can be achieved in a meaningful way.

The second purpose ongoing feedback serves is to place value on the process of learning and creating. The traditional model for homework and projects places the sole emphasis on the final product. Think about the typical science fair where students conduct a science experiment at home, create a display board, and share what they did; the students' grades are all based on what they showcase at that moment, which, in turn, sends the message that all that matters is what they produce. Value should be placed on final products, but it is doing our students a disservice to ignore the journey taken to learn the material.

The Struggle Is the Point

Another way we can support our gifted middle schoolers in combating their perfectionism is through our curricular design. I already mentioned that I used projects and assignments to provide ongoing feedback, but there are additional ways we can adjust our classes. Choosing content that addresses the specific skills we want to develop is a powerful way to give support in this development. For example, one of the first projects I would conduct with my history class was to have the students explore the failures of one of their heroes.

The project was titled "Why Do We Fall?" after the quotation from *Batman Begins* (Nolan, 2005), and I asked students to create a research presentation about one of their heroes. The catch was that they were not allowed to focus on the successes of that hero, but rather, needed to tell us about how they failed. While the content-based goal of this project was for students to develop and demonstrate their ability to do research, it also served as a reinforcement of the struggle that every successful person goes through. As students gave presentations about figures like Steve Jobs and Bill Watterson, it allowed us to celebrate failure, and understand that even the people we look up to the most fell short at some point.

In addition, being deliberate with the content we choose is important for challenging students and allowing opportunities for direct discussions about struggle. There is a sweet spot with the resources we use with our students, and it can be difficult to find the right balance. Too easy and the students will be bored; too hard and the students will feel discouraged. We are looking for those resources that provide a meaningful challenge but are still accessible. Just selecting the right materials is not enough, however, as there still needs to be active metacognitive discussions about the process of learning.

The first novel I would read each year with my gifted middle school students was *Fahrenheit 451*, Ray Bradbury's dystopian novel (1953) about a world where books are burned. The content of this book was engaging for students and allowed for some very meaningful and relevant discussions relating to the current world, but Bradbury's writing was often difficult for students to understand on a first read. Selecting this novel first was deliberate, as it challenged students, while also demonstrating for them how rewarding working through the struggle could be. As we held discussions about the book, it was common for students to have moments of clarity where they finally understood what they read the night before. We did not stop there, though, and made a point of discussing the factors impacting their understanding. As students would share their struggles, others would chime in with their agreement, while others would share different issues they had with the text. We would then brainstorm strategies they could use to gain a better understanding of the book.

This strategy is not just about selecting challenging materials, but also underlines the importance of engaging with the students. Without our discussions about what was hard to understand about Bradbury's writing, the students would be left feeling abandoned as each one thinks they are the only ones not understanding the book. Instead, by opening a dialog, students can see they are not alone. Sometimes this would develop naturally, with a student sharing something specific they found difficult, while at other times I would initiate the discussion by sharing something I personally found challenging in the writing. This opening created an opportunity where students did not feel awkward sharing their experience. This contributed to the culture of the class, while also equipping them with strategies they might not have developed before middle school.

Another way we can support students in embracing struggle is by encouraging them to get involved with clubs or sports they might not have joined otherwise. In many middle schools, there are district organized sports, and these are great opportunities for students to get involved. In the district where I taught, middle school sports were part of a festival season, meaning that any student who joined got to practice with the coaches and compete in a district-wide tournament. From there, the top team was selected, but every student had the opportunity to play and be part of the team for most of the season. Throughout my time teaching at the school, I coached three different sports, and I always encouraged my students to participate.

These sports were great in helping gifted students manage their perfectionistic tendencies, because, for many, these were games they had never played formally. While not every student would make the All-Star team, I established early on that my goals for them were to have fun and improve, even if it was just a little. For some students this was difficult, but we used practice as an opportunity to debrief about their frustrations.

Another value of getting students involved in sports like this is because they provide a natural opportunity for goal setting, which is a strategy that can be used with gifted students to combat perfectionism, in a non-threatening environment (Winebrenner & Brulles, 2018). Since perfectionism is centered on a vision of attaining the unattainable, by helping to create manageable goals, we assist in developing a critical skill for our students, especially since any lofty desire is comprised of countless smaller goals. For students to whom school has always come easy, the idea of creating these smaller benchmarks can be difficult; however, since sports are so skills-based, it allows for very direct and deliberate progress to be visualized while also allowing for differentiation of individual players' goals.

When I would coach basketball, the conversations I had with each player were incredibly different. I would have one player whose goal was related to shooting while another player was working on not flinching when they were trying to get a rebound. In each of these cases, the students were working toward the final goal of creating a winning team, but their individual journeys were unique. These skills are transferable to the classroom and can help students understand that their worth is not tied to being perfect.

This Burger Looks Nothing Like the Picture

When I would teach creative writing, one of the foundational principles is the idea of showing versus telling. While we can tell someone that Captain America is brave and has a good heart, it is another thing to see him jump on a grenade to protect his friends. The feelings we have when experiencing something are far stronger than those we have just hearing of them, and this goes beyond literature. When we have somebody saying that they will act one way and then they do the opposite, the pain we feel is amplified, and this is the reality of our middle school students. When we tell them we don't expect perfection, and that the struggle is something to be celebrated, we need to live by those words. For example, if a teacher starts the year by celebrating a growth mindset, encouraging students to take risks and not get caught up on getting the right answer, but then criticizes the class when it is taking longer than expected to learn a skill, then the message is clear that the only thing that matters is results.

This same message can be sent to our students when we do not embrace our own personal mistakes.

There is something about becoming a teacher that is incredibly intimidating. Each day we stand in front of our classes, sharing content and having interactions that will have an impact which will last a lifetime. We can inspire and change lives. We can make kids feel cared for and safe. I'm at the point in my career where some of my earliest students have graduated from college and are making an impact on the world. One day while I was driving, I was listening to NPR (National Public Radio) and the reporter for the story was a former student. After experiencing the roller coaster of emotions ranging from "Oh gosh, I am so proud of this student" to "Oh my gosh, a former student is writing for NPR … I'm getting old," I thought about who that student was when they first set foot in my class.

Being a teacher means you are literally shaping the future, and that is incredibly scary!

I think every person has their own educator who made a positive impact on their lives that they will remember forever. It might have been what the teacher taught or how they made the student feel, but there is something about them that lasts forever. These teachers from my own life have made an impact on the way I teach, as I try to live up to the mytho-logical pedestal I have built them in my mind. As we strive to live up to the example set by our educational idols, we can fall into the same pitfalls of perfectionism as our gifted students.

This can be incredibly detrimental to the classroom relationship. For example, in a 2021 column discussing the role of authenticity and gifted identity development, Tracy Cross identifies multiple examples of gifted students struggling with inauthentic interactions, and concludes by stating the overt need for adults to be authentic (Cross, 2021). Gifted students are perceptive, so they will notice when mistakes are made, and if they are covered up or lied about, this can be incredibly damaging. This also applies to our curriculum, as many gifted students have an extensive know-ledge about a lot of topics. They will ask questions and make corrections in the middle of the class if they see an error. This can be embarrassing, but when teachers don't acknowledge the corrections or try to argue that they are right, it not only hurts the relationship, but models for our students that they should not admit to making mistakes.

As teachers, it is important that we embrace our mistakes in order to model for our gifted students that everybody makes errors. Now, this is not an excuse for coming unprepared for class or not knowing the content, but if you say something incorrect or don't know the answer to a question, embrace it! In my time teaching there have been many occasions when a student has asked something I did not know the answer to, and, if the question is on topic, my response is usually, "I don't know the answer to that. Could you look it up and report on it for the rest of the class?" This little action goes a long way in validating our student's curiosity, while also demonstrating that not having all the answers is not a bad thing. In fact, this models for them how to move forward when they are faced with not knowing it all.

In working with gifted students for more than a decade, I have never experienced kids disrespecting a teacher who was honest about not having an answer or admitted a mistake. It is easy to be intimidated and worry that our classes are looking for perfection; that they will take out Mary Poppins' magic tape measure to see if we are "practically perfect" (Stevenson, 1964). The reality is they are not looking for perfection; they are looking for you to be genuine. In fact, most of the conflicts I've seen between gifted students and teachers have derived from teachers challenging a correction or refusing to acknowledge a mistake. These standoffs never go in favor of the teacher and cause a transition in the power dynamic. By acknowledging that we do not have an answer or asking students to verify a point, we empower them, validating their questions or knowledge, while also ensuring that the correct information is shared with our class.

Another way in which we can demonstrate that it is alright to make mistakes and not be perfect is by taking our own risks. Trying new things in our classes or participating in school events we wouldn't normally take part in are great ways to engage with our students and model this important skill. In 2012, when I was teaching the gifted self-contained class, I read an article about how to use a Nintendo Wii controller to create a SMART Board on any surface with a projector. I thought this was something the class would find cool, so I purchased all the necessary components, and set about trying to make this work. When I explained to the class why there was a Wii controller taped to the projector, they were all very excited, but when we had the big unveiling, it was a giant disaster. None of it worked the way it was supposed to, and I had 30 middle schoolers watch as I frantically tapped on the wall trying to interact with the screen. Instead of being embarrassed, however, I asked my students to troubleshoot the problem, and leaned on their expertise. Eventually we got the interactive screen to work. Comparing it to a SMART Board was like comparing the picture of a fast-food burger to what you get in the wrapper, but it was this shared moment of struggle we were all able to overcome together.

Summary

Perfectionism is a problem that can plague gifted students. While the foundations are often established when students are younger, as content becomes more complex in middle school, the pressures of being perfect can begin to grow exponentially. As teachers, we have an important job in supporting our gifted students in developing a positive self-concept, as our messaging can either reinforce perfectionistic tendencies or help students realize that perfect is not realistic. By celebrating the process of learning and the struggle that comes with it, we help to reinforce what it really means to learn. In addition, we need to model for our students that we are not perfect and let them see how we overcome problems caused by our mistakes.

Reflection

1. When was the last time you took a risk in your classroom? For an upcoming lesson, incorporate one risk that might not turn out the way you expect.

References

Besnoy, K. D., Jolly, J. L., & Manning, S. (2011). Academic underachievement of gifted students. In J. A. Castellano & A. D. Frazier (Eds.), *Special populations in gifted education: Understanding our most able students from diverse backgrounds* (pp. 401–415). Prufrock Press Inc.

Blitz, J. (Director). (2009, February 1). Stress relief (No. 86) [TV series episode]. In *The Office*. NBC.

Burns, S., & Horhager, M. R. (Directors). (2019, November 12). Playdate with Magenta (No. 2) [TV series episode]. In *Blue's Clues & You!* Nickelodeon.

Cross, T. L. (2021). Social and emotional development: The role of authenticity in the psychosocial development of students with gifts and talents. *Gifted Child Today*, 44(2), 111–114. https://doi.org/10.1177/10762 17520988777

Delisle, J., & Galbraith, J. (2002). *When gifted kids don't have all the answers*. Free Spirit Publishing.

McKay, A. (Director). (2006, August 4). *Talladega nights: The ballad of Ricky Bobby* [Film]. Sony Pictures Releasing.

Merriam-Webster. (n.d.). Definition of perfectionism. Retrieved August 5, 2022, from www.merriam-webster.com/dictionary/perfectionism

National Association for Gifted Children. (n.d.). Perfectionism. Retrieved August 5, 2022, from www.nagc.org/resources-publications/resources-parents/social-emotional-issues/perfectionism

Nolan, C. (Director). (2005, May 31). *Batman begins* [Film]. Warner Bros. Pictures.

Silverman, L. K. (1997). The construct of asynchronous development. *Peabody Journal of Education*, *72*(3/4), 36–58.

Stevenson, R. (Director). (1964, August 27). *Mary Poppins* [Film]. Buena Vista Distribution Company, Inc.

Winebrenner, S., & Brulles, D. (2018). *Teaching gifted kids in today's classroom* (4th ed.). Free Spirit Publishing.

Putting It into Practice

In the *G.I. Joe* TV series from the 1980s, episodes would feature a public service announcement (PSA) to help educate viewers on important life skills like not to lie or get in cars with strangers. These PSAs followed a similar structure, with a brief scene followed by one of the *G.I. Joe* members explaining the lesson. After the explanation, one of the children would inevitably say, "And now we know," to which the *G.I. Joe* character would reply, "And knowing is half the battle" (Thompson et al., 1983). Until this point, we have focused primarily on understanding the needs of gifted middle schoolers, but that is only half the message. In every one of these situations, action is needed to do the right thing, and, just like the children in the PSAs, just knowing about the social-emotional needs of our gifted middle school students is not enough.

While we have discussed some ways in which you can support gifted middle school students in developing their identities, this chapter will focus on strategies you can use in your classrooms. I have personally implemented all the strategies and lessons suggested in this chapter, so I will be sharing my experiences. There is no one-size-fits-all solution to meet the needs of your gifted middle schoolers, but these examples should aid you in developing ways to address your specific situation. My goal is for you not just to feel empowered but also supported in taking action to guide students in your classes.

DOI: 10.4324/9781003332015-5

What the Research Says

Before diving into specific strategies, it is important to understand the ways in which teachers and schools impact adolescent identity development. While the question "Who am I?" is very personal, it is also affected by various external factors and experiences. Considering that at least one-third of a teen's day is spent at school, it is important to understand how schools impact, both positively and negatively, an adolescent's identity development. Researchers Verhoeven, Poorthuis, and Volman (2019) conducted a literature review of 111 different studies, and identified three different ways in which schools impact adolescent identity development: unintentionally, intentionally, and with the preconditions to support identity development (Verhoeven et al., 2019).

There were several different considerations regarding the unintentional ways in which schools and teachers impacted this phase, many of which negatively affected adolescents as they developed their identity (Verhoeven et al., 2019). First, selection practices can have a clear impact, where admittance and acceptance to different programs and extracurricular activities can positively or negatively impact student engagement and perception (Barnett, 2006; Solomon, 2007; Yi, 2013). Along with this, expectations can play a significant role; in one study, a teacher's low expectations negatively shaped a student's perception of themselves as a math learner (Heyd-Metzuyanim, 2013). It is also important to understand that peer norms are a factor that can unintentionally impact identity development. In another study, it was found that a student was unable to assume a new role and classroom identity in the class because of established social norms (Fields & Enyedy, 2012).

The findings from studies where schools intentionally impacted identity development were interesting, as the majority of them focused on activities outside of the normal school day (Verhoeven et al., 2019). While not directly tied to classroom practice, there are still many valuable lessons to be learned from this research. For example, in a section discussing literature addressing "In-Breadth Exploration," Verhoeven et al. noted that providing opportunities for "on-site" and "hands-on" activities empowers students to see themselves in these different identity positions (2019). The final consideration from the literature review were the factors that lead to identity development. In this section, they note two key ideas, "meaningful learning experiences" and a "supportive classroom climate" (Verhoeven et al., 2019, pp. 52–54).

While each of the studies highlights a different element or consideration of how schools impact adolescent identity development, there is a clear conclusion: school is an important place where students are discovering and considering who they are and could be. As educators, we owe it to our students to do everything we can to be supportive in this process.

There's a Lesson There Somewhere

With the limited class time we have, the thought of adding another task to our overflowing plan books can make us want to scream. I have seen this happen countless times when district or school initiatives are presented, and the stress begins to show itself on each teacher's face as they try to figure out how to make it work… or worse, they simply write it off as something that will change in a week. However, if we are strategic, we can use the lessons we are already teaching to reinforce identity development in meaningful ways. There are two different ways these lessons can be developed: through content or through skills.

Content describes the specific topics covered in a class, including state standards, adopted curriculum, and district-approved texts. Since these already need to be covered, mining them for as much content as we can just makes sense, especially if we consider that gifted students need depth and complexity in what they learn (more on this in Chapter 5).

To utilize content for identity development, the first task is to analyze the objectives we must cover. For example, when I was teaching 7th grade gifted literature, I deliberately combed through the district-approved reading list to identify texts that would resonate with my students. While I had not read every text on the list, I talked with the other English teachers, getting their feedback on what themes were addressed in the novels, as well as those which resonated with their students. In addition, I also independently researched the different texts for plot and theme summaries. This work was something that I would naturally do as an English teacher, but I was deliberate in considering the ways in which the texts would resonate with my gifted students.

For history, it was a similar process, but a bit more abstract. The American Revolution was a standard for 8th grade history. It was a topic

I had to cover, and, while there were specific performance objectives the students needed to address, I still had the flexibility to find opportunities for depth and complexity. In framing my American Revolution unit, the theme of causes worth fighting for was apparent, and allowed students an anchor to relate the content to themselves. In addition to learning about the specific events and figures of the Revolution, my students were also considering the causes they felt were worth fighting for. So much of integrating identity development into your classroom comes through the way you frame your content. By doing this, it becomes relevant.

Skills, on the other hand, are more generalized, and reflect the processes through which students learn. Where content represents the specific details like identifying all parts of a plant cell or discussing all the provisions in the Bill of Rights, skills are often the ways in which students learn the content, like understanding cause-and-effect relationships in history. These are much more flexible than content when it comes to working in your classroom, and by understanding the skills students need to have, projects and activities can be developed to reinforce these *and* develop gifted middle school identities.

Examples

I want to share with you two lesson examples I have used in my classroom to reinforce identity development. While these lessons are course specific, my hope is that they will inspire you in designing your own identity-enriched lessons.

Content Example – The Outsiders: *A World Unknown*

This first example is a culminating project from a study of S. E. Hinton's novel *The Outsiders*. I used it with gifted 7th graders, and when I would survey the class about their favorite novel at the end of the year, this was usually the top pick.

The novel takes place in the 1960s and focuses on two rival gangs: the greasers and the socs (short for socials). The story is told through the perspective of Ponyboy, a greaser who is involved in the death of a soc, and he and his best friend go into hiding. Through his experience, Ponyboy reflects on who he is, as well as learning that there is more to the socs than he assumed (Hinton, 2006). One of the central themes of this novel is identity, so it worked as a powerful piece for this age group.

As a culminating project, I asked students to tell us about a world they experience that none of their classmates understood. This project mirrored the novel, as the reader discovers at the end that Ponyboy too was recounting his experience for a class assignment (Hinton, 2006).

The project had two central components. Students needed to create a product, using any medium they wanted, to share with the class something they experienced that the rest of us would not understand. For the second part, students needed to write an explanation comparing their experience to that of Ponyboy, utilizing evidence from the text. The goal with this writing assignment was for students to move beyond plot-based comparisons and consider the larger theme of identity.

Since this project happened during the 4th quarter, there was an existing culture of trust amongst the class, and students were willing to be incredibly vulnerable in what they shared. Even if the class was aware of some of the things shared, often they were unaware of the extent to which these experiences shaped their peers. Throughout the years of doing this project, students shared many powerful worlds with the class: one student explained the amount of work they put in as a competitive gymnast, another shared their experience with managing Type I Diabetes, and another discussed being autistic.

One student I had, nearly a decade ago, shared a project that has stuck with me all these years. They were a very talented artist, and when they stood up to present, they brought up an illustration of three different plants: one blooming fully, one shriveled, and one blooming again. They shared with the class that because they were part of a military family, they moved across the country often. As a result, they did not spend much time in one location. They explained that the three different plants represented who they were and their experience with moving so frequently. The fully blooming plant was how they felt when they were comfortable and had spent enough time somewhere to feel like themself. The shriveled plant was who they were when they had to move, having to start over at a new place. The plant mid-bloom represented who they were as they started to feel more comfortable again. They explained that this cycle was one that had happened regularly, but they were learning from each experience.

In each of the student projects on *The Outsiders*, they demonstrated to me that they understood the themes of the novel, but more importantly, they demonstrated a deeper understanding of who they were. In middle school, a time when conformity is common, the class members were able to consider themselves as individuals while also celebrating their peers.

Skills Example – Your Story Thus Far

The second example addresses the ways we can use the skills we are naturally developing in our classes to support gifted middle school students. This approach is more flexible than content-based assignments, but it does require a stronger understanding of the nuances within the standards and objectives. It is also important to consider the impact these projects will have on the flow of a class, as time needs to be dedicated for students to complete each component. For content-dense subjects like history or science, assignments like these can feel disconnected from the material taught. Careful planning is required to consider what skills are needed, the timing for implementing the project, and the way that implementation interacts with the rest of the content.

The example project, "Your Story Thus Far," served as an introductory assignment for my history class. This course utilized the Cambridge International Curriculum history syllabus, which is a similar program to Advanced Placement or the International Baccalaureate program, and I wanted to preassess a skill – asking students to understand historical concepts like cause and effect and the perspectives of those in the past (Cambridge Syllabus 0470). Although this skill would naturally be addressed in the content-focused units, I thought it was important to isolate it without influence from background knowledge. What this meant was that this time was not being allocated for students to work directly on syllabus content during the project. As a teacher, this can be difficult to grapple with, as class time is incredibly limited; however, gaining information on specific skills does allow for more focused differentiation to occur. It is a delicate balance that requires specific and detailed planning.

To focus on the desired skill, I had the students share about a subject they knew better than anybody: themselves. The parameters of the project were straightforward, as students had to identify and share three key events from their life as well as explaining how they ended up in the gifted history classroom. Students could demonstrate these events in any way they wanted, and were encouraged to let themselves be seen in the final product. In order to assess their projects, the rubric reflected the ways in which students applied the skills rather than focusing specifically on the content.

The products students have turned in for this assignment have been incredibly diverse, and have truly reflected each individual. By allowing such diverse methods of expression and subject matter, my gifted students have truly provided me with an understanding of who they are, while also demonstrating their specific strengths and needs in terms of the course learning objectives.

Celebrating Student Interests

In addition to adjusting our curriculum, there are specific things we can do outside of our lessons to help support identity development in our gifted middle schoolers. These non-curricular strategies require very little effort on our part, but they can go a long way.

The first thing we can do is to show an interest in what our students value. I have had many gifted middle schoolers who, when they find something in which they are interested, tend to dive in headfirst, consuming and learning as much as they can. There is a passion that comes with these interests, and they become something that students feel deeply about. This intensity is not unfounded, as that is one of the common descriptors of gifted students. In considering Dabrowski's overexcitabilities (McWilliams, 2019), this characteristic makes sense. While Dabrowski does not explicitly address the concept of fandoms or other interests, we can see these trends are there. For example, an intellectual overexcitability is characterized by curiosity and great focus on areas of interest (McWilliams, 2019). While we may want to write off new interests as phases or something they won't care about in a week, for our gifted middle school students, these interests are part of their development as individuals. By acknowledging these, we not only help to develop a positive culture, but we also validate their identities.

It is easy to feel disconnected from what adolescents today care about, but you do not need to know anything to show a genuine interest. I once had a student who loved the *My Little Pony* TV series reboot. They talked about it regularly, and not knowing anything about the series, most of it sounded to me like they were speaking a different language; however, that did not stop me from asking them about the show. Questions as simple as how the show was different than the 1980s version went a long way in giving them an opportunity to share with me, while I worked to gain a better understanding of them. As the year progressed, they started sharing with me different things that were happening in *My Little Pony*, and while I still did not understand the series, these were simple moments which showed that my interest had made an impact.

Connections with student interests do not take any significant time but allow your interactions to be much more meaningful. As I walk through the halls at my current school, I have brief, regular conversations with students about their passions, and the topics vary wildly. In a typical day I will speak with one student about the Phoenix Suns and immediately switch to talking about Taylor Swift with another. These check-ins might not seem like much, but just like placing money into a savings account, they grow and compound over time.

Classroom Traditions

Another way to share your interests with your students is through small traditions. These little moments can add up in a big way and help draw direct attention to your interests. These traditions don't have to take up a lot of time and can work in the background, so they are not intruding into your day-to-day classroom operations.

For example, I love the Arizona Diamondbacks baseball team. One year, at the start of the season, I placed the team's record on the board. This was not obtrusive but was situated next to the day's agenda. Students started to notice, and if I forgot to update the record, the students would ask if they could change it. This eventually shifted into a task my first-period students started rotating through, and many would check the record to make sure it was correct. Most of my students did not care about baseball, but they were able to see that it was important to me. For those who did follow baseball, it provided another opportunity for them to connect with me and see that liking sports did not prevent them from succeeding academically.

Another example of integrating your passion through a tradition is something I saw another teacher demonstrate. This teacher taught a self-contained gifted 6th grade class and loved The Beatles. Every Friday she would have "Beatles Friday," where she would only play Beatles music while the students worked. This became something the students connected with, and even though many of the students did not start as Beatles fans, when they came to my gifted 7th grade class they would ask if we could keep the tradition alive. While we would play Beatles music on Fridays, it was not authentic to who I am, so I added a day that spoke to my interests: "Tay Tay Tuesday," where I would play Taylor Swift music every Tuesday. This was not only authentic to me, but created a platform for students to share their own musical tastes. Throughout my years of teaching, I have had students who loved Taylor Swift debating with students who did not, students advocating for "One Direction Wednesdays," and a more general openness about musical taste. Students whom I would not have assumed would be friends found connections over common interests.

Let Your Inner Geek Out

If I have learned anything from watching cartoons in the 1990s, it is that you must be true to your heart. Films like Disney's *Mulan* and *Aladdin* had this message at their core, with the heroes only able to resolve the central conflict after they accepted who they were. Although this message is tossed around frequently, I still see teachers not being themselves in front of their students. While there is a level of professionalism that needs to be maintained, letting our own interests shine in the classroom models for our students that it is alright to be yourself.

Just as for our students, this can be an intimidating prospect. I have seen many TikTok videos of an educator sharing the ways in which their students savagely made fun of their lunch or haircut, and while this never feels good, if the classroom culture is built effectively, these challenges can be minimized. If you establish that the culture in the class is one that builds each other up and there are best intentions, then students will naturally carry this forward. It is important to note, as well, that this does not mean the classroom is a sterile environment without fun or laughter. The students in my classes feel comfortable and will give each other a hard time, but they are careful about not hurting their peers. If a line is crossed, with the culture we have established, the class often jumps in to support each other before I can.

Like so many things in education, this is something that needs to be modeled. Students need to understand not only where the line is, but how to react if they feel hurt. My classroom is typically very fluid, with an emphasis on student discussion, so there is a natural flow that comes with this. In addition, just like with this book, I tend to relate content to my own life or through a lens my students might understand more clearly. As a result, I have had many moments where we laugh together about something silly I have done, and this will often result in comments from the class. When I told my classes that I was writing this book, for example, they were overjoyed, but they also gave me a hard time. They made jokes about the content that should be included (they were very adamant that I include a reference to the website "Ducksters") and the means by which they would obtain a copy (I had to have an overt discussion of the way royalties work). Sharing this project with them was an incredibly vulnerable moment, but something they needed to see.

As we have these brief discussions, I make sure to set the tone, laughing along, but also identifying when I feel the class is pushing a boundary. I am typically overt with this, saying something along the lines of, "I know we're not trying to be mean, but the comments are feeling more critical than supportive. Let's try to keep everything positive." This is especially beneficial for gifted adolescents as gifted students tend to have a heightened sensitivity (McWilliams, 2019). Comments or actions that might be written off by most people can result in a deep analysis and dissection to ascertain if there is any element of truth. This can take up a great deal of their mental space, as students to try to figure out if they are actually being made fun of, or if their peers are just having fun with them. By modeling advocacy skills in this way, it helps them develop their voice and realize what they can say if something makes them uncomfortable.

As the leader in your class, modeling who you are also helps your students see that your personal passions supersede any judgments that come with them. One of the easiest ways that you can do this is through the way you decorate your classroom. While having content-appropriate posters and decorations is important, there are usually spaces where you can share your own interests. Posters, pennants, pictures, etc., are all ways that not only showcase who you are, but also make the classroom feel more like home.

Reading this, it probably seems obvious that decorations are a way to share your interests with your students, but the impact this has can be profound. When I was teaching the self-contained gifted middle school program, I went all out with having things that I loved as the decorations in my classroom. In addition to the traditional history and literature posters, I filled my walls with superhero memorabilia, action figures, cutouts of comics strips, and movie posters. Walking into my classroom, there was no doubt I am a giant nerd. This was around the time of the first *Avengers* movie release, so most of my classes were excited to see giant cutouts of Iron Man and Marvel Pop Figures. It was not uncommon for times when students moved between classes to be filled with speculative discussions about upcoming movies or superhero cameos.

While this made most of my students feel comfortable and established a positive culture, there is one student who stands out from my experiences. This student would regularly participate in our class pop culture discussions, but I never thought much of it. At the end of the school year, they gave me an end-of-year gift. I started by reading the card, and this student wrote me a long message, thanking me not for the content we learned, but for helping them to feel comfortable being themself. They explained that when they came to middle school, they thought they had to stop liking and playing with action figures. Thinking they were too old for that, they did not display the toys they loved; however, after being in my class, they realized it was alright to still like those things and put their toys back on the shelves. This was a child battling with who they were as well as what they loved. Thinking in terms of asynchronous development, this was a student who, intellectually, was thinking well above a 7th grade level, but still had likes and interests of somebody younger. This is common in gifted students, as their intellect and development are out of sync, and it can cause confusion and frustration (Silverman, 1997). I never had an overt discussion with this student about being themself or not caring about what others think. I just shared what I loved, letting them see themself in what I did.

Summary

Identity development is so important for gifted middle school students, and it is crucial that we consider the ways that we can support this. Through developing content-based and skills-based lessons, students can have opportunities to explore who they are while still meeting curricular goals. In addition, through the simple act of being ourselves, we demonstrate for our classes that what an individual loves and cares about is important, regardless of what others say. In doing this, we can make students feel comfortable in discovering who they are.

Reflection

1. Review your curriculum (either lessons you've already taught or lessons you plan to teach) and consider what opportunities there are for students to explore who *they* are? How can you adjust your curriculum to allow for self-expression and consideration of their identity?

2. How much of *you* is present in your classroom? How much do your students know about your interests and passions? Is there a way you could share this with them the next time you see them?

References

Barnett, L. A. (2006). Flying high or crashing down: Girls' accounts of trying out for cheerleading and dance. *Journal of Adolescent Research*, *21*(5), 514–541. https://doi.org/10.1177/0743558406291687

Fields, D. A., & Enyedy, N. (2012). Picking up the mantle of "expert": Assigned roles, assertion of identity, and peer recognition within a programming class. *Mind, Culture, and Activity*, *20*(2), 113–131. https://doi.org/10.1080/10749039.2012.691199

Heyd-Metzuyanim, E. (2013). The co-construction of learning difficulties in mathematics: Teacher–student interactions and their role in the development of a disabled mathematical identity. *Educational Studies in Mathematics*, *83*(3), 341–368. https://doi.org/10.1007/s10649-012-9457-z

Hinton, S. E. (2006). *The outsiders*. Viking Books for Young Readers.

McWilliams, C. (2019, February 8). *Why can't they loosen up? Intensities of gifted youth*. Gifted and Talented Education. Retrieved from http://gate.outreach.msu.edu/about/226/why-cant-they-loosen-up-intensities-of-gifted-youth

Silverman, L. K. (1997). The construct of asynchronous development. *Peabody Journal of Education*, *72*(3/4), 36–58.

Solomon, Y. (2007). Experiencing mathematics classes: Ability grouping, gender and the selective development of participative identities. *International Journal of Educational Research*, *46*(1–2), 8–19. https://doi.org/10.1016/j.ijer.2007.07.002

Thompson, D., Gibbs, J., Lennon, T., & Lee, R. (Directors). (1983). *G.I. Joe: A real American hero* [TV series]. First-run Syndication.

Verhoeven, M., Poorthuis, A. M. G., & Volman, M. (2019). The role of school in adolescents' identity development: A literature review. *Educational Psychology Review*, *31*(1), 35–63. https://doi.org/10.1007/s10648-018-9457-3

Yi, Y. (2013). Adolescent multilingual writer's negotiation of multiple identities and access to academic writing: A case study of a Jogi Yuhak student in a US high school. *The Canadian Modern Language Review*, *69*(2), 207–231.

It's Elements of Differentiation, My Dear Watson

Literature is filled with iconic examples of gifted individuals, but I think one of the strongest is Sherlock Holmes. Sir Arthur Conan Doyle's 1891 creation took the world by storm and popularized the modern detective story for the world. With superior intellect and keen reasoning, no problem was outside of Sherlock's skillset, and just like his partner Watson, readers followed along in awe as he deduced solutions based on the smallest details. Holmes was described in such vivid detail that fans even wrote letters to the fictional detective into the 1980s, believing he was real (Green, 2016).

When teaching gifted middle school English, my unit on Sherlock Holmes was one of my favorites. Not only did I get to share some of my favorite stories with my students (when I was in high school, I started a club where we read mystery novels; it was called "The Baker Street Irregulars," named after the group of children Holmes employs to gain underground information), but I also got to see a whole new generation of kids be challenged and amazed, just like I was. Even more special, though, was watching them see themselves in Holmes. They identified with both the good and the bad, and we used this as a platform to talk about what it means to be gifted. As an educator, I realized something I never did when I was just reading the stories: he needed differentiation.

Tomlinson and Allan define differentiation "as a teacher's reacting responsively to a learner's needs" (2000, p. 4). While it is common to think of needs as deficits or areas for growth, the term also refers to strengths and topics mastered. As for Sherlock Holmes, there is a reason he was not part of the police force, and he only accepted cases he found particularly

DOI: 10.4324/9781003332015-6

interesting: simply solving mysteries he already knew the answer to provided him with little mental stimulation. He preferred to reserve his time for problems that would challenge and push his thinking. Many of our gifted students are just like this; they know the answers and understand the content, but they need more. They are looking for challenge and stimulation, and a curriculum that meets them where they are.

They need differentiation.

One Size Doesn't Fit All

A common myth associated with gifted education is that gifted students will be fine on their own. As many gifted students are performing academically above their age peers, there is the misconception that these students do not need additional support. State and federal mandates require students to reach proficiency, and it is understandable why teachers focus their attention on students who have not yet reached those levels; however, this practice completely ignores the needs of students who have already achieved mastery. Every student deserves the opportunity to come to school and be challenged, learn something new, and engage with content in a different way.

Imagine an 8th grade science class with a content focus on biology foundations. The teacher, to understand their students' proficiency with the material, gives a pre-test at the start of school that covers every topic that will be seen throughout the year. If a student achieves 95% on that assessment, what can that student hope to get out of the class? They have already demonstrated that they have mastery of the material, and while there is that extra 5% they could achieve the next time they take the test, how much can they really expect to learn if there are not any adjustments made to the curriculum?

By differentiating, we acknowledge and respond to our students' needs, meaning those who need extra support and those who need extra challenge (Tomlinson, 1999). To do this, we need to understand who our students are, and make meaningful, focused adjustments. By doing this, our classrooms can truly be a dynamic place of growth and development for *all* students.

Vin Diesel Would Be Proud: Fast and Furious Acceleration for Gifted Students

Before addressing the ways in which teachers can differentiate their curriculum to meet the needs of all learners in their classes, it is important to understand the role acceleration plays in supporting gifted students. Throughout popular culture, grade- and content-based acceleration is actively represented. For example, the 1990s TV series *Smart Guy* and *The Big Bang Theory* spinoff, *Young Sheldon*, both feature elementary school prodigies who skip grades to be in high school since their academic needs are not being met.

The term "acceleration" is used when students move through the curriculum at a faster pace than their grade-level peers. Even within this definition, there are various ways it can manifest, including "grade-skipping, early entrance to kindergarten or college, dual-credit courses such as Advanced Placement and International Baccalaureate programs and subject-based acceleration (e.g., when a fifth-grade student takes a middle school math course)" (National Association for Gifted Children, n.d., para. 1). Advancing through the content creates natural layers of complexity as it becomes more difficult. Since students are not spending time repeating skills they have already mastered, their engagement is aligned with their intellectual level.

Acceleration does have challenges that come with its implementation. First, since gifted students are advancing through curriculum at a faster rate, there are important considerations that need to be made regarding the maturity of the content. This reminds me of the late comedian Mitch Hedberg, who joked, "Every book is a children's book if the kid can read" (Hedberg, 2003). While the general idea of this joke is sound, it does ignore the role comprehension and emotional maturity play in the reading process. Throughout its content scope and sequences, the curriculum is ideally laid out in a way that acknowledges not just the intellectual aspect. With acceleration, this aspect needs to be carefully considered, especially when asynchronous development is factored into this equation. Being a humanities teacher, I have found that the history and reading content can be incredibly complex and meet the students where they are intellectually; however, there are times that the content is out of sync with where they are emotionally. The classics are filled with incredibly powerful messages, but also include content that might not be appropriate for adolescents. When acceleration is utilized to support gifted learners, this is a consideration that needs to be addressed.

Another component of acceleration is the impact on long-term academic planning, logistics in scheduling, and transportation. As students move through curriculum at an accelerated rate, this naturally has a bigger impact on that student's overall academic trajectory. While the traditional school system moves sequentially, with content building on itself from grade to grade, when students advance through this structure in an unconventional way, adjustments need to be made. This can be especially challenging if that student is completing subject-based acceleration, but not matching that acceleration in other content areas. For example, if a student is extremely gifted in math and is completing middle school math in 4th grade, it needs to be considered what will happen when that student moves on to high school math. Questions like whether the student will take geometry on the high school campus or online need to be considered, as well as the way the student's schedule is impacted when the high school day starts earlier than that of the elementary school. How will the student get to and from the high school? What plans will be made when the student completes the high school math curriculum?

While acceleration seems simple on paper, it does require long-term planning. As a result, all key stakeholders should be involved in the discussions to make sure gifted students are supported. Some key figures for inclusion are the student, the parents, the administration, the classroom teacher, school and/or district gifted educators, and teachers from the next grade levels. While this seems like a lot of people to be involved, it is much better to identify and address these questions early on rather than wait for a barrier to cause a disruption in a student's academic path.

Elements of Differentiation

When considering differentiation within the classroom, there is no better place to start than with the work of Carol Ann Tomlinson. Her expertise on the subject is foundational in the field of education and has been a driving force in supporting not just gifted students, but all students. Through understanding the unique learning needs of the students in our classes, we can provide substantial and meaningful instruction.

There are four distinct elements we can differentiate for our students: content, process, product, and the learning environment (Tomlinson, 1999). Each of these elements works together to represent the foundations of effective instruction, and in adjusting these elements, our classrooms can be more conducive to meeting the unique needs of each student.

Content

Content represents what students are learning (Tomlinson & Allan, 2000), which, for most subjects, is guided by state and national standards. Often, these standards are assessed using state and other high-stakes exams. This often creates a push-and-pull factor, where educators feel pressured to make sure that only content which will appear on the state assessment is covered in class. For gifted students, however, it is important to understand that, while they are learning the same content, they will often learn it quicker than their age peers, if they do not already have mastery. Differentiation of content becomes crucial, as it ensures that they are not just sitting in a class bored or not being productive. As we consider how to differentiate our content for gifted learners, we should be looking at providing opportunities for depth and complexity in the subject (Tomlinson & Allan, 2000).

While the standards are valuable in providing a guide for what students should learn, they should never be looked on as restrictive. Instead, consider them as a baseline. If students are below standard proficiency, support should be provided to help them reach that level; however, if students are already demonstrating proficiency, we need to consider how we can help them understand these standards at a deeper and more meaningful level (Winebrenner & Brulles, 2018). For example, when I taught 7th grade history, one of the state standards required students to understand the causes of the American Civil War. This objective is straightforward, and students could simply memorize the five events and explanations the state identified. However, to differentiate content, I referenced Bloom's Taxonomy (Winebrenner & Brulles, 2018, p. 145), considering the top three levels, and pushed students to understand the causes and motivations. This was at the analyze and evaluate stages of the taxonomy. I wanted students to be able to judge the actions of the past, weigh the impact of the different events on the overall cause of the American Civil War, and defend their conclusions about the causes of the war. While this might not seem like much, it was the deliberate consideration of my gifted students' needs that drove the way I framed the content.

Process

Process is directly tied to content, and reflects *how* students learn the material (Tomlinson & Allan, 2000). One important point to note is that process is unique to every student, and students will work at different levels of readiness, with different interests, and their unique learning profiles (Tomlinson, 2001). If we think about a class of 30 students, it is hard to imagine a scenario where every one of those students would learn the content in the same way at the same level. Even in the self-contained gifted classes I have taught, the students all approach learning in different ways. Some want to dive into discussion, arguing and thinking on the fly; others want to spend time gathering information to organize their thoughts before sharing; still others want to create something that applies their thinking in a way to make sense of what they have learned. Regardless of the methods, the process should reflect the students.

When considering process with gifted middle schoolers, one of the core ideas is to ensure that the content is higher order in nature, with an emphasis on complexity (Winebrenner & Brulles, 2018). Establishing this creates a scenario where students need to make sense of information, gathering and sharing sources to come to meaningful conclusions. In many ways this consideration can be connected to asking closed versus open-ended questions. If we ask questions that are too direct, the work students will put in will match this level.

One fear that I have heard expressed about differentiation is that it means writing 30 different lesson plans – one for each student in each class. That is not the case. Differentiation represents an awareness of and responsiveness to students, and then making adjustments to meet these needs. The modifications do not have to be time-consuming to have a large impact on students. Even something as simple as giving options as to how students access the content (watch a video, read an article, etc.) can make a huge impact on their abilities to access the curriculum. We will talk more in Chapter 6 about the components that can inform differentiation decisions.

Product

Product represents the ways in which students demonstrate their learning (Tomlinson, 1999). Tomlinson explains that this element of differentiation is larger than the process, and should be reflected over a long period of time, like a unit or a semester (Tomlinson, 2001). Through products, students get the opportunity to showcase their learning and understanding, and there are a variety of ways this can be demonstrated.

It is important when discussing product to also consider assessment. While some include this as its own separate category, the products we ask students to complete should all be part of ongoing formative and summative assessments. While it is easy to think of the test at the end of a unit as the only assessment, everything we ask students to do during a unit should be informing our understanding of how students are thinking and learning. All products that students complete should play a role in this process and be building to support the overall practice of learning.

Both formative and summative assessments play a valuable role in our classrooms, but I want to highlight the role formative assessments play in working with gifted students. As we have talked about already, goal setting and emphasizing growth are important factors in supporting gifted learners when dealing with perfectionism. The way we use assessments also contributes to this, as placing value on the formative assessments, the process of learning, helps students see that there is more to school than just the grades they earn on a test. If the content and products are differentiated, then the ongoing formative feedback helps to guide students in developing their thinking and considering the ways in which they have grown throughout the process. If, however, the activities students complete are at a lower level and the final unit test is all that matters for the grade, then the message is clear to students that the test is all that matters. Every day should hold value for our class, to drive and develop their thinking, and the products and assessments we use are core factors in this.

Learning Environment

A final element of differentiation is the learning environment (Tomlinson, 2003). We've talked a lot about the environment of our middle school classrooms and the ways in which we can build culture, but the learning environment also reflects responsive practices to the needs of students. In describing this element, Tomlinson also uses the term "mood," and notes that every part of what students do is impacted by the environment (Tomlinson, 2003). This can be represented by providing more support to students who need it, while giving those who crave independence freedom; providing students who need silence with a quiet learning environment, while those who need music to focus have the freedom to listen to music on headphones; allowing students to work independently or in groups (Tomlinson, 2001). At the core, the learning environment needs to be conducive to the needs of the students.

For gifted students, there is an added layer of establishing our expectations for the level and ways in which they learn. Considering the other three elements, if the content, process, and product are asking gifted students to dive deeper into curriculum, working at the higher levels of Bloom's Taxonomy, we need to create a learning environment that embraces these factors. Students should not feel at odds with what is being asked and the ways in which we support them in reaching those goals.

Differentiation in the Middle School Classroom

While the elements of differentiation are foundational across grade levels, I think it is important to emphasize what this looks like in a middle school classroom. One of the immediate challenges that comes with implementing these strategies is time. In a typical middle school classroom, a teacher has approximately an hour (usually less) to work with each class, and they will typically have close to 200 student contacts. This combination of short time and growing numbers of students can be daunting, but by using each element of differentiation as a foundation, meaningful differentiation can occur. This section will look at the elements of differentiation and consider the ways in which a middle school teacher can effectively meet the needs of their gifted students.

Learning Environment

To craft a differentiated middle school classroom, I think it is important to start with the classroom environment. Since each class is unique, this provides an opportunity to allow the identity of each class to drive the ways in which the other elements of differentiation are presented. In addition, by establishing early on the high expectations we have for our gifted students as well as our emphasis on the learning environment, we allow our students the opportunity to influence the content, process, and products.

One of the first ways in which we can establish the learning environment is by addressing our expectations with our classes from the very beginning (Winebrenner & Brulles, 2018). While there are the natural ways that we model these ideas for our students, I find it highly effective to directly explain what I expect from my students, and I will typically write this in my syllabus. Since the beginning of the school year is spent reviewing expectations and the syllabus is the foundation of the class, by writing it here, it clearly communicates to students and parents the tone of the class, and the nature of the learning environment.

For example, in the section of my syllabus about grading, I provide an explanation detailing *formative* versus *summative* assignments, along with my reasoning as to why they are both important. Early in the school year, students, parents, and I are all on the same page as I emphasize that the process of learning is more important than the final grade. In addition, in the introduction section for the class, I also highlight the collaborative and project-based nature of the class. Early on, students can ask questions about the nature of the class and gain an understanding of what I would like to see throughout the year. Frontloading all these elements provides a strong and meaningful foundation.

Another aspect of the learning environment is the physical makeup of the classroom. The way desks or tables are arranged sends a clear message to students about the ways in which they learn. If we want a collaborative space, the layout of the classroom should reflect this. Arranging desks in pods of four tells students that they will need to interact with their peers at some point. Contrast this with columns of desks all facing the board, which sends a message that they will be hearing lectures from the teacher and working independently. It is important to reflect not only on the type of class environment you want, but also the one your students need.

Content and Process

While content and process are two distinct elements of differentiation, there is value in discussing the two together. Content is the foundation of everything we teach, and it is important that we have a strong understanding of each of the objectives. This content, however, is a more general catch-all term to refer to what is being learned in the class. As we consider the ways in which we differentiate, one of the most important distinctions we can make with content is to discern between skills-based and content-based objectives.

Skills-based objectives often refer to the foundations of learning, which in many ways are the basis for accessing later content. For example, students need to be able to read and reason to comprehend and discuss later topics. Content-based objectives, on the other hand, refers to the specific facts, figures, or concepts under a given discipline. I've often heard this described as the distinction between the primary grades where students learn to read versus the secondary grades where students read to learn. While this is an incredibly simplistic way to assess these ideas, it helps frame what students are learning. In addition, I think it is important to note that these two elements (skills and content) are not mutually exclusive, and I believe students should be developing both at all grade levels. The reason I bring this up is because as we consider differentiating content, each of these elements combines to support our students.

For example, using the Arizona History and Social Science Standards, there are five different categories identified: Disciplinary Skills and Processes, Civics, Economics, Geography, and History (Arizona Department of Education, n.d.). As a teacher referencing these standards, the distinction between the skills-based and the content-based objectives is important and provides a meaningful place to start differentiating. While every student might be learning the same history topics, the objectives and modalities for learning can be different. By using skills as the foundation, it allows students to access the content in very different ways that support their individual learning needs.

The Arizona History Standard 7.SP1.1 asks students to "Analyze connections among events and developments in broader historical contexts" (Arizona Department of Education, n.d.). This skill is direct in what it is asking students to accomplish, but the expected outcome is wide open in terms of what students could produce. Although Arizona students are primarily learning 20th- century history in 7th grade, the standard is left open enough for students to consider connections beyond just the scope outlined. One of the goals with differentiation is to push students in their thinking and understanding, and not feeling restricted by the standards is one way to do this. For standard 7.SP1.1, gifted students could be asked to connect the developments of the history content being studied to their lives today, or consider how the developments being studied connect to areas not immediately being studied. This understanding opens the standards so that students at varying levels can learn the same content, while developing in ways that meet their needs.

Product

The products that students submit are important as they are the manifestation of what students have learned. As we teach and guide our students, we want the result to be reflective not just of what they learned, but be meaningful in the process. In addition, as we consider the skills-based and content-based objectives, we want to make sure any product can tie back to at least one of these elements.

Where this becomes a challenge for middle school teachers is the sheer number of students we have. Using 200 student contacts as a base, that means 200 individual sets of feedback, guidance, and support. This can be an immense time investment from the teacher, and if we are looking for prompt and impactful feedback, potentially require commitments of time outside of school.

The first consideration is how we design our products. While it is typical to feel the need to have an assignment at the end of each lesson, the depth and complexity of these lessons need to be considered. Some of the questions we should be asking as we develop assignments are: is the lesson just a reinforcement of the content shared in class or is it developing skills the student needs? What value will the students find in this assignment? Is this assignment authentic to the field I am teaching? While every assignment cannot answer every one of these questions, they do provide a basis for us to meaningfully consider how they will impact our students. In considering our gifted middle schoolers, if students do not find value in what they are doing, this can create challenges in the classroom, as some gifted students will choose not to submit assignments because they do not see the point. Delisle and Galbraith distinguish these students from underachievers, describing them as "selective consumers" (2002, p. 167). In addition, if gifted students can choose not to complete work, but still get an A on the final assessment, this sends the message that the assignments are not supporting or developing the skills they need to be successful.

Another way to support differentiation while also alleviating some of the time impact is by providing consistent feedback and support throughout the process. My classes tend to be project-based in nature, so students have a lot of independent time where they are working on and developing their final products. During extended work times, I make a point to conference with every student/group (often visiting them wherever they are working in the class), providing feedback, asking questions, having discussions about the content, and working to push them in their thinking, whatever their level might be. These conferences are incredibly valuable for two reasons.

First, it allows me to assess where every student is in the process of learning, as well as gaining an understanding of the challenges (or lack thereof) they are facing. This fills in the understanding I would gain by giving students an assignment on the topic but allows for more direct and immediate feedback. When we assign our students a task and they turn in the assignment, providing immediate feedback is more impactful for student learning (Opitz et al., 2011). I have found this point to be especially true if the assignment is content-dense. For example, if I assign my students a Web Quest to identify causes of the American Civil War, and wait a week to provide feedback, chances are we have moved on as a class from that subject. That means the feedback the students are receiving does not hold any immediate value for them unless we are very direct in the feedback we provide.

In addition, by having these direct conversations with students, it empowers me to differentiate the content and process on the fly. For example, using standard 7.SP1.1, I can assess student thinking very quickly, and guide them in directions I feel will support their needs. If a student is struggling to make connections, I can guide them to resources or topics that will allow them to demonstrate the skill; on the other hand, if I have a student who sees the immediate connection within the content, I can guide them to expand their thinking, challenging them to make bigger or deeper connections.

You Did It! Now Do It 20 More Times

One of the most important things to consider when differentiating product for gifted students is that it is not simply adding more work. One of the classic examples used to demonstrate this is giving the class ten math problems; if a gifted student completes them before the rest of the class, it is not differentiation to ask them to do the next ten.

While this seems obvious when it's presented so directly, in practice I can understand why this is the go-to reaction. As educators, we understand the value of repetition to gain mastery. How do you get to Carnegie Hall? Practice. While there is value in having gifted students practice, the reality is they require fewer repetitions and iterations than their age-level peers (Winebrenner & Brulles, 2018). This is an important understanding for all age groups, but for gifted middle schoolers, this is especially important, as, from my experience, their understanding of the value of their own time is more pronounced. I've had many gifted students choose not to complete assignments because they had something "better" they needed to do or they did not find value in the assignment. If students show they have mastered a concept, if we simply ask them for more of the same, we are essentially telling our students we do not value their time.

What we should be aiming for is to provide students with work and content that addresses the core concepts while being challenging enough to engage them. The rigor we ask for should not come from the quantity of the work, but rather, the quality and depth.

Summary

Differentiation is one of the most foundational elements of education, and something we truly need to master if we are going to support gifted middle school students. Through differentiated content, we are not only able to engage our class, but help them to grow. Differentiation takes time, understanding of the individuals in your class, and a willingness to not have every student in your class working on the same activities. Through this chapter we discussed the foundational elements of differentiation, which are critical. By framing what we do with these ideas in mind, differentiation becomes more natural and straightforward.

In the next chapter we will look at more direct ways for implementing differentiation within your class. With each of the strategies discussed, please consider this chapter and the four core elements of differentiation, focusing particularly on how the strategies discussed connect to these elements.

Reflection

1. Review the four elements of differentiation. Which of these elements do you feel you do a good job at differentiating? Which do you need to improve?

References

Arizona Department of Education. (n.d.). *Seventh grade: Integrated global studies*. Retrieved August 13, 2022, from www.azed.gov/sites/defa ult/files/2019/04/Seventh%20Grade%20One%20Pager%206.10.19. pdf?id=5caf9e881dcb2511e88cfe28

Delisle, J., & Galbraith, J. (2002). *When gifted kids don't have all the answers*. Free Spirit Publishing.

Green, A. (2016, March 8). Who answers Sherlock Holmes's fan mail? Mental Floss. Retrieved from www.mentalfloss.com/article/76722/ who-answers-sherlock-holmess-fan-mail

Hedberg, M. (2003, December 9). *Mitch all together* [CD]. Comedy Central.

National Association for Gifted Children. (n.d.). Acceleration. Retrieved August 10, 2022, from www.nagc.org/resources-publications/gifted-education-practices/acceleration

Opitz, B., Ferdinand, N. K., & Mecklinger, A. (2011). Timing matters: The impact of immediate and delayed feedback on artificial language learning. *Frontiers in Human Neuroscience*, *5*, 8. https://doi.org/ 10.3389/fnhum.2011.00008

Tomlinson, C. A. (1999). *The differentiated classroom: Responding to the needs of all learners*. Association for Supervision and Curriculum Development.

Tomlinson, C. A. (2001). *How to differentiate instruction in mixed-ability classrooms* (2nd ed.). Association for Supervision and Curriculum Development.

Tomlinson, C. A. (2003). *Fulfilling the promise of the differentiated classroom*. Association for Supervision and Curriculum Development.

Tomlinson, C. A., & Allan, S. D. (2000). *Leadership for differentiating schools & classrooms*. Association for Supervision and Curriculum Development.

Winebrenner, S., & Brulles, D. (2018). *Teaching gifted kids in today's classroom* (4th ed.). Free Spirit Publishing.

Let There Be Dinosaurs!

In 1989, whether he knew it or not, Bill Watterson, author of the comic strip *Calvin and Hobbes*, created a comic that demonstrated the need for differentiation more clearly to me than any textbook I read in college. In the comic, the father is tucking his son in for the night, and shares that he and Calvin's mom are disappointed in the child's report card. He states that the two of them feel like their son could do better, to which Calvin replies, "But I don't like school" (Watterson, 2012, p. 319).

This surprises Calvin's dad, as he explains that his son loves to read and learn things. He goes on to remind Calvin how much he has read about dinosaurs and that learning is fun. He then asks Calvin why he doesn't like school, and Calvin simply replies, "We don't read about dinosaurs" (Watterson, 2012, p. 319).

We don't read about dinosaurs.

Such a simple statement that describes the experiences of so many gifted students. Across the United States there are so many Calvins; students whose parents get report cards or emails saying that their child is failing physics, but this leaves the parents confused as they have seen their child spend hours listening to astrophysicist Neil deGrasse Tyson. These are children who fail papers requiring them to analyze themes in *Great Expectations*, yet can talk at length about the role ambition plays in the anime *Naruto*. These are students who fail history tests, yet can argue about the significance of figures like Hercules Mulligan and the Marquis de Lafayette in the musical *Hamilton*.

This chapter is designed to help not just the Calvins, but all gifted students, as differentiation plays a critical role in reaching this population.

DOI: 10.4324/9781003332015-7

While Chapter 5 addressed the foundational elements needed to differentiate, this chapter focuses more closely on the practical ways you can implement this in your classroom.

When considering differentiation, Tomlinson identifies three factors that influence this practice: readiness, learning profile, and interest (Tomlinson, 1999). By referencing and understanding these components, meaningful and focused decisions can be made regarding the four elements of differentiation discussed in Chapter 5.

Readiness

Readiness describes where a student is at in terms of mastery and understanding the content (Tomlinson & Allan, 2000). If we think about a typical class, our students are going to approach the content from a range of levels, with varying degrees of background and understanding. In my time teaching history, I have had incredible disparities in my class, as some students enter it not knowing anything about World War II other than Germany was our opponent, and others enter the class having watched every documentary the History Channel had to offer. This range of abilities can be incredibly challenging, and it is a natural tendency to focus our attention on those students who need the most support; however, in assessing readiness, we consider all this information and adjust our curriculum to meet the varying needs of our students.

Assessments

It's all well and good to understand that we need to vary our instruction to meet the unique needs of our students, but how do we get this information? With so many students in our classes, it can be a daunting task to try to figure out where each student is in their understanding of the content. By using formal and informal assessments, we can be responsive to our students' needs and use the data that we gather to directly guide our instruction.

Preassessments with each unit provide a powerful snapshot to understand where each of our students is in terms of what we are going to teach. One of the standard ways in which preassessments are used is to track growth throughout a unit. At the start of a unit, give students an exam that has no impact on their grade to determine what they know, and then, at the end of the unit, give a similar assessment to see how much growth was achieved. This are powerful data, but we need to make sure we are doing something meaningful with that information.

In my first year of teaching, my school had a training on "LtoJ" charts, which is a way of understanding the progress our students make throughout the year. The concept is this: if you graphed your class's knowledge at the beginning of the school year, the graph would resemble an "L," with most students not knowing the information and clustering on the left-hand side of the graph. Halfway through the year the graph would look more like a standard bell curve, with a more natural distribution. At the end of the year, the graph would resemble a "J," since the majority of the class would have gained mastery of the content and be clustered on the right-hand side of the graph (LtoJ Consulting Group, n.d.).

As a new teacher, this all made sense, and I was very motivated to see that progress throughout the year; however, I was part of a teaching team, and the science teacher had a different perspective. When our team met, we were discussing this professional development session, and they let out an expletive-filled rant about how ridiculous the training was. "Of course, the graph is going to change! I didn't teach them anything and then I taught them! No..." You get the idea.

My team member had a point; the trend of the data is what we should be expecting in our classes throughout each unit. By the end, most of our students should be at a level of proficiency that shows they are ready to move on. Where I do feel my colleague was off course, however, was the idea that these data served no purpose. While simply identifying what our students know or do not know does not have much of an impact, using that data to guide our instruction can not only positively impact our students, but also make us more efficient and effective teachers.

The use of preassessment is a key component to differentiating by readiness (Winebrenner & Brulles, 2018). By having data to support what students know and do not know, we are able to tailor our instruction to meet the needs of the class. As a history teacher, if my students all know the provisions of the 13th, 14th, and 15th Amendments to the U.S. Constitution before I start my American Civil War unit, why should I spend time directly instructing or assigning work that simply repeats content they already know? Instead, that time could be spent learning other content they don't know or exploring questions they have.

At the middle school level this is especially important, as the content becomes more complex. The skills and knowledge students learn at middle school have so much opportunity for engagement, but there is a lot of content to cover in one year. By using preassessment data to assess readiness, we become strategic with our content and the time we spend in class.

This can also drive placement decisions for students to receive additional support. Many middle schools have honors programs that provide content at a faster pace or with more depth and complexity. By having preassessment data for the year, recommendations can be made for students to be placed in these classes. While not a perfect solution to addressing the challenges facing gifted identification, this is another resource for supporting students who might not have been identified to receive the services they need.

Preassessments in Practice

When designing preassessments, it is crucial that the assessment is reflective of the goals of the unit. Using the standards as a guide, the questions should connect the content and skills you need to address. Your goal should be to understand at what level each student comprehends the content before instruction. Once we have these data, we then adjust our plans to meet the students where they are. This helps in two ways. First, it allows us to avoid covering ideas or skills most of the class already know or have. While we are addressing differentiation in terms of supporting gifted learners, differentiation is a practice that is beneficial for *all* students. Second , there are specific data regarding the strengths and weaknesses of each student.

This practice is foundational in the *Cluster Grouping Handbook (CGH)* by Winebrenner and Brulles (2008), which covers ways to provide gifted services and support in heterogeneous elementary classrooms. While the book addresses specifics about arranging grade-level classes in a way that disperses gifted students to allow for more focused differentiation, the strategies that Winebrenner and Brulles present can also be applied at the middle school level. While the master schedule might dictate the grouping of students, the differentiation strategies they discuss are still applicable in 7th and 8th grade classrooms.

For example, one of the strategies discussed is the use of Renzulli's curriculum compacting, which is essentially allowing gifted students to spend more time on work that is challenging rather than the grade-level curriculum (Winebrenner & Brulles, 2008). Essentially, by knowing what students know and need to know, you can move through the required curriculum at a more accelerated pace, thus opening opportunities to engage in more complex material. By using preassessments, you will easily be able to identify those students who are able to compact the curriculum, participating in extension or enrichment activities, and those who need more direct support (Winebrenner & Brulles, 2008).

Another strategy Winebrenner and Brulles recommend that coincides with the "readiness" element of differentiation is the concept of "most difficult first" (MDF) (2008, p. 42). In this strategy, after presenting an introduction to the material, when students begin working on the accompanying assignment, allow those who feel they have mastery of the content to complete the hardest problems from the practice. If students can get four of the five correct, then that demonstrates mastery and they can move on to the extension activity (Winebrenner & Brulles, 2008). The thinking with this strategy is that if students can demonstrate understanding with the hardest problems first, then they do not need to repeat that process with the easier ones. This strategy works best with skills-based assignments, rather than content-based ones, since iterative practice is a foundation of skill-based content. In addition, it is very important that the problems selected for the practice actually represent the hardest options students would be expected to complete at the end of a unit, as this serves as a demonstration of mastery.

One of the core ideas we need to understand when using preassessments to differentiate for our gifted students is that these opportunities are not exclusive to our gifted students (Winebrenner & Brulles, 2008). This is not a concept where the gifted students get pulled aside to take the special assessment, but rather, it allows all students the chance to show mastery of content if they feel confident.

When I was a student teacher in a 5th-grade gifted cluster classroom, my mentor teacher helped me to design a unit utilizing the pretest as an opportunity for extension activities. This concept was very powerful – to see that there were students who were not identified as gifted who already had mastery of the content, as well as gifted students who did not have that same mastery. Through that unit, every student was able to get what they needed, and I was able to let data drive my decisions. Another aspect that my mentor reinforced was that differentiation is not a punishment or a reward for knowledge, but rather, an opportunity for every student to be challenged at the level they need. The students who did not meet the threshold on the pretest did not feel ashamed, knowing they had opportunities to grow in that specific skill; the students who worked on the extension activity did not brag or rub it in their peers' faces, because they understood that all the class was learning the same core content, just in a different way.

The pretest data also give the teacher specific language and data for communication with parents and students. In this digitized world, students (and their parents) have more access to information about their grades than ever before; a student's grades are no longer a mystery. In my experience, when parents sit down for a parent–teacher conference, they do not want you to simply review the grade book; rather, parents want details about their child's progress, where their strengths and weaknesses lie, and how we are working to address those needs. Sitting down for a parent–teacher conference and explaining how a child performs on preassessments, the ways they tackle extension activities, or their progress on completing the most difficult problems first is incredibly powerful.

Extension Activities

Extension activities are a concept that Winebrenner and Brulles address in the *CGH*. The idea is that when students demonstrate mastery over the grade-level content, they will "extend" beyond the parameters of the grade-level objective (2008). These should be activities that coincide with the topics being addressed, while allowing students to dig deeper into the content. Using Bloom's Taxonomy as a foundation, extension activities should focus on students synthesizing the information and forming judgmnts. The process should be higher order in nature, driving students to think deeper about the content.

Extensions at the Middle School Level

A challenge with extensions at the middle school level is that the social dynamics do play a part in the ways in which students will achieve as well as the comfort they feel engaging in these activities. As we have already discussed, there is research to support gifted students hiding their abilities in order to fit in with their age-level peers. This can be incredibly challenging to deal with, especially when the goal of extending the curriculum is to provide deeper understanding of the content beyond what the traditional curriculum might offer.

One way to address this is through the culture and climate we set regarding curriculum and extensions. The tone and wording we use are very important, as we do not want to create an environment in which completing the pre-test with an A makes students feel uncomfortable and those who do not pass feel inferior. The goal of differentiating based on readiness is to ensure that students are being challenged at their level with the same content base. The tone we use in introducing the pre-test and extensions needs to emphasize this point. If an administrator or parent came through the class and asked students to explain what was happening, each student should be able to explain the reasoning behind this strategy.

Another aspect to this is the nature of the assignments we create for our students. We need to ensure that there is not a giant discrepancy between the engagement and enjoyment offered by the extension activity and the grade-level activity. If students who pass the pre-test get the opportunity to make a movie while the rest of the class must complete worksheet questions, it's no wonder this might create feelings of division and exclusion. *Every student* deserves high-quality and engaging activities and we cannot let differentiation be an excuse for not giving our students meaningful things to do.

When I was student teaching, I had to meet with other teacher candidates and my university advisor to debrief on how our student teaching experience was going. This meeting was a simple discussion of the highs and lows of our experience, and there was nothing noteworthy about it. There was one teacher candidate, however, who has forever been burned into my mind. During our discussion they said, "I hate my gifted students." I couldn't believe what I was hearing for several reasons. One, what kind of teacher hates *any* student? Two, when student teaching in a gifted cluster classroom, how could you hate such fun and quirky kids? This student teacher continued by explaining that they felt the gifted students thought they were so special because they finished their work early and then got to go on the computer and play games. They thought this was not fair to the rest of the class.

In looking back, while I still cannot believe a teacher would ever say they hate a single student, let alone a whole population of students, I feel bad that this was their experience with gifted students and differentiation. Clearly their mentor did not explain to them that differentiation is not a carrot we hang in front of students to make others feel bad. In teaching, we should aim to have every student impacted by every lesson. While there is a place for focused, pen and paper practice, that should never be used as a perceived punishment.

Another consideration with differentiating based on readiness is your role as the teacher. It can be easy to assume that since certain students have already demonstrated proficiency on a particular skill, they are good to be left alone to work while direct attention is paid to those who have not mastered the content. This could not be farther from the truth, as we need to be supporting every student. The nature of that support might change, but we should be actively working with our entire class.

When students are working independently and applying skills, this is the perfect time to meet with them, have focused conversations, ask questions, etc. Typically, in my classroom, there are large chunks of time when students are working independently or in small groups. During this time, I rotate between all students, checking in, asking questions to probe their understanding, giving feedback, and being an active partici-pant in their learning. When students are working at different levels, these conversations don't single out individual students since I am having them with all students. What is unique, though, is the nature of the discussion, and that is driven by student readiness.

As we consider these conversations and feedback, I do warn you not to move in the same rotation every day. As middle school teachers, our time is very valuable, and in a 45-minute class, it is amazing how quickly time can pass. If we rotate through conferencing with our students in the same order in every class, that can create a situation where the last group gets less time than their peers, often significantly so. I am especially guilty of this, as I tend to get very enthusiastic about discussing content with students, so the five minutes I set aside for each group creeps past that. As a result, I try to be conscientious as to how I meet with groups, rotating through whom I meet with first so that every student gets focused time with me. If you have students working at three different levels based on a pre-test, make sure that your extension activity students are not always last.

A final consideration with differentiating based on readiness is how gifted students can feel if they do not pass the pre-test. I have seen pre-tests implemented in classrooms with great intentions, well-planned activities, and a deep knowledge of each student's level of understanding. While the meaning behind the plan was great, the response from gifted students who did not pass the pre-test was anything but. They felt offended they were not able to do the extension activity and argued with the teacher about the test. Some students wanted to retake the preassessment to prove that they actually knew the material, while others were just frustrated. In this case, while everything was executed well with the implementation, an unexpected main problem was timing. It was the 4th quarter, the first time a differentiation strategy like this had been rolled out. The students did not know how to respond, because this was completely different from the way the rest of the class was organized.

With any big changes, it is important to make sure we are clear in how we frame them and build on our established culture. This should coincide with deliberate planning to ensure activities are not designed in a way that makes them feel like a punishment. Finally, the language we use to describe this design should support these points and work to build our students up during the vulnerable time that is middle school.

Learning Profile

The learning profile reflects the ways in which individuals learn (Tomlinson, 1999). While the word "profile" might conjure up images of in-depth documents outlining how each individual student learns, it is much simpler than that. By simply understanding the preferred ways in which students like to learn, we can provide opportunities to engage with the curriculum in this preferred way. While the learning profile will touch on all the elements of differentiation, it is especially present in the learning environment and the process.

For the learning environment, the design and feel of the classroom are major factors that can influence how students feel within a class. Their ability to access curriculum can be heavily influenced by factors such as the noise level or the ways in which students are able to situate themselves. Even small changes, like ensuring that students have the freedom to move throughout the classroom during work time, can make a huge difference.

Another factor we need to consider are group dynamics (Tomlinson, 2001). By understanding whether students prefer to work with small groups, big groups, or by themselves, we can ensure there are opportunities that support this learning need. One aspect to consider with groupings for gifted middle schoolers is that many dislike group work (Winebrenner & Brulles, 2018). Even if they have come from self-contained programs, it is not uncommon for them to have experienced a system where other individuals do not complete their designated section of the work, and the main responsibility has fallen on them. As we design our curriculum, we need to be attentive to this concern of gifted students, especially when it comes to the learning profile. While it is important to help students push outside of their comfort zone, we also need to be attentive and supportive with building any group dynamics. This includes establishing guidelines for individual roles and what to do if students are not meeting their individual responsibilities.

Another consideration is the ways in which students learn. Tomlinson identifies several considerations such as the modality (auditory versus visual), the way information is presented (starting with the big picture versus introducing small pieces), and the varied intelligences (Gardner's Multiple Intelligences) (Tomlinson, 2001). Adjusting the curriculum based on learning profiles can be incredibly fun, and it is one of the reasons I always tell my students that I rarely have two groups learning the same content in the same way. For example, I had one group of students who loved debates, and they excelled at challenging each other in a respectful way; on the other hand, I had another group whose members were so supportive, they rarely challenged each other. As I designed lessons for the two different groups, I needed to account for these differences, and modified the curriculum to best support their unique learning needs.

One of the points Tomlinson makes about the learning profile is the importance of realizing that we will have different profiles than many of our students (Tomlinson, 2001). It can be easy to assume that our way of doing things is the best, but if our students need silence to be able to process while we typically listen to music, we need to make the adjustments that are best for our students. One way to establish this early is to survey your students about how they learn. Through Google Forms, a survey tool utilized through the Google Workspace, students can note the approaches they have to learning, and we can work to ensure there is flexibility in the classroom environment that accounts for these distinct learning differences.

Interest

My favorite way to differentiate is based on interest. Think about a time when you were really interested in something, and the amount of focus and dedication you devoted to that topic. It could be a hobby or just something you're curious about, but there is power in passion. I know for myself, when I am passionate about something, it creeps into all aspects of my life. Fortunately, my wife knows and appreciates this about me, as she has had to sit through many explanations about the manga (Japanese comic) *One Piece* or the card game *Magic: The Gathering*.

Our gifted students are the same way and come to the things they love with a high level of intensity and passion (Webb, 2016). The internet has only enhanced this, as students can now find entire communities focused on the things they love. Go to Reddit and there is pretty much a message board filled with passionate people dedicated to any topic you can imagine. Students are no longer limited to people in their class or books in the library; the world is opened to them! With the entirety of human knowledge held in their smartphones, the limitations of the classroom can be incredibly frustrating.

For the Calvins of the World

Think about a child like Calvin from the comic strip described at the beginning of this chapter. Calvin struggles in school, yet has a near encyclopedic knowledge of dinosaurs. He is a child who, under traditional metrics of education, would not be considered a high achiever, yet he demonstrates all the traits of giftedness. His teachers are failing him, yet the world only sees a mischievous child who does not do well in school.

I've had many Calvins throughout my time teaching. They can be frustrating for parents and teachers, as the dedication they show to their interests demonstrates they have the capacity to do great things, but that same passion is nowhere evident in the class. It is frustrating for the student as well; in many cases, they are aware of their abilities and know what they are capable of, yet see and feel the frustration they are causing to the people around them. While school is an agreement between students and teachers that teachers will teach and students will learn, we have a responsibility, as educators, to do what we can to meet the needs of these students.

The inspiration for this book was a presentation I gave in 2021 at the NAGC Annual Conference titled "When Calvin Goes to Middle School." In it, I detailed many of the same concepts addressed here, but the pop culture references were restricted to just *Calvin and Hobbes*. The reason for this is that I have seen many Calvins come through my classroom who had enormous potential yet struggled. They were kids with whom I connected, talked about their favorite things, and let them be themselves. I tried to find ways to tie in their passions, connecting *The Avengers* to history or Taylor Swift to Edgar Allan Poe, all in an attempt to tap into all that potential.

As you read through this section, please think about the Calvins you currently have in your class or have had in the past. What was that spark for them? What did you hear them talk about with such passion you were in shock at how much they knew? While sometimes a passion might be a square peg to the round hole of our curriculum, there are many ways we can make things fit. We can reach these students.

As you read, think about how you can help the Calvins in your world.

It Starts with a Question

Before we dive into the more challenging task of connecting random topics into your content area, it is important to define the term "interest." When we consider student interest, we might first think of personal passions, but there is more to it than that. Interest reflects the topics a student is curious about or something they wonder (Tomlinson, 1999; Tomlinson & Allan, 2000). There are a lot of different avenues we can use to tap into their interest, and one of the easiest is finding out what students want to know about a topic.

The KWL chart (Cash, 2017, pp. 74–75) is a standard way of assessing understanding and interest, but it can hold a lot of power if we encourage students to engage with the chart in a meaningful way. If you are unfamiliar with a KWL chart, the "K" stands for "What we already know about the topic" (this is also a really good form of preassessment), the "W" stands for "What we want to know," and the "L" stands for "What we learned." These charts are nothing new in the realm of education, but I tend not to see them implemented at the middle school level. I am not sure of the exact reason for this, but if I had to guess, it would center on the amount of content we need to cover coupled with the short time frame we have with each class. While this does take time out of our busy schedules, utilizing the KWL chart gives us a foundation to tie each unit back to student interest.

Richard Cash presents another way of utilizing student interest through his KIQ charts; the acronym represents "what I *Know*, find *Interesting*, and have *Questions* about" (2017, pp. 74–75). This emphasis on interests and the questions we have about a topic can be a meaningful change to the standard chart, while also emphasizing that there are still questions we might have, even if we already know a lot about a topic (Cash, 2017). Regardless of which method is used, engaging students in getting thinking about a topic is very powerful.

At the beginning of a unit, I will usually have an introduction, something to get the kids excited about what we will be learning. This can be a video clip, a quotation, or even just me setting the stage. After this introduction, I will have students write down what they are curious about, encouraging them to think beyond just facts, as we will cover those naturally throughout the unit, but also not limiting them to one area of curiosity. Imagine being an adolescent, finally excited about a topic, and you're told you get one question. It is important that, as educators of gifted adolescents, we are not the source of a student's passion being extinguished.

There are times when what students want to learn is completely outside of what can realistically be covered in 7th or 8th grade. I have seen this happen many times in science classes, where student curiosity slingshots straight to college-level content. These sorts of situations warrant a one-on-one discussion with that student to understand what they want to know, and more importantly, how you can help them learn it. When I have had these discussions, one of the biggest concerns has consistently been gaps in student understanding. A student wants to know about astrophysics, but does not understand the basics of Newton's Laws. In these instances, I will usually outline the skills or content they need to show mastery of before tackling such a big question. If those basics are set up as a foundation, then it can help fuel the progression for a student getting to learn what they want to learn (the pre-test can serve as a good foundation for this discussion). What is important is that what the student needs to demonstrate is not framed in a punitive manner or in a way that makes them think we do not believe in them. Students should know these skills are necessary for them to fully understand and appreciate the higher-level content.

The second important part of having student questions be part of our engagement is to make sure we act upon them. If we simply ask students what they want to know about a topic and never come back to answer their question, then why should they be invested in future lessons? In these scenarios, we are asking them to help shape our classroom, and it is critical that we validate their input. Even if a question is covered through a discussion or lecture, by acknowledging the student interest chart or the question an individual might have asked, it helps show the students that their thoughts and considerations are part of our plan. For those questions that are not part of our standard curriculum, this is a great opportunity to have students research independently or in small groups to find answers. This empowers them because they are providing solutions to their questions, but also helps to support them in deepening their understanding of the content.

Let There Be Dinosaurs

When we talk about integrating student interest into our curriculum to differentiate, it is easy to immediately think of what students like, whether inside or outside the classroom. These passions have a way of shaping our understanding of the world. The Netflix series *Stranger Things* is a perfect example of this. Set in the 1980s, the show focuses on citizens of a small town dealing with the supernatural disappearance of a boy named Will. He and his friends fit into the stereotypical representation of "nerds," doing well in school, playing Dungeons and Dragons, loving fantasy stories and comic books, etc. As his friends try to find out what happened to Will, they encounter monsters and secret organizations, and to make sense of these things, they frame them in terms of comic books and Dungeons and Dragons (M. Duffer & R. Duffer, 2016). Many of our gifted students are like this, and if we can tap into this passion, we can help them connect with the content of lessons in incredibly meaningful ways.

To do this, we need to be comfortable taking the scenic route in reaching our curricular objectives. When we differentiate by allowing students to pursue interests, at times these connections to curriculum can be disconnected from the general flow of what we need to teach. This essentially means that we must fit in additional content on top of what we are already teaching. While this might seem like an impossibility, the act of forming these connections helps to reinforce the content we need students to learn.

Having taught English for years, this is probably the easiest subject area to tie in student interests. Because the objectives tend to be skills-based, this allows for a great deal of individualization in terms of what materials we use to reinforce those ideas. It is important, though, that any modifications or additional materials you integrate coincide with district policy.

What do we do, though, if the subject we teach is content-based? There are still those opportunities for differentiation based on interest; we just need to be creative. For example, imagine you have a student like Calvin, who is obsessed with dinosaurs, in your 7th grade social studies class. How do you connect dinosaurs to World War II?

In a situation like this, I would start by brainstorming anything and everything associated with dinosaurs. This brainstorm becomes the base from where I try to find some thread that connects to my content area. In thinking about World War II, the topics that I immediately connect with dinosaurs are art museums and fossils. Using those base words as a foundation, I can then connect to the ways the Allies worked to preserve works of art in museums, trying to keep them from being destroyed or taken by the Nazis. This is a topic I would naturally bring up in my history class, but there is a new avenue to consider: while the Allies protected pieces of art, what did they do with the fossils and dinosaur bones?

This question provides a great opportunity to engage a dinosaur-obsessed kid, as it connects directly to the content but also places value on what they do. Any student who finds this topic interesting could research what was done, connecting to the discussion in a unique but meaningful way. Students could even move further up Bloom's Taxonomy by arguing whether enough was done to protect the fossils in comparison to artwork.

While this might appear tangential, that is alright, as to go off on these tangents, students need to understand the surrounding materials. While they are researching dinosaurs in World War II, they need to understand the motivation of the Nazis in taking priceless pieces of artwork. This ties to Hitler's goals as a leader, which were reflected in the ways in which he attained power. To understand this, students need to understand the state of Germany and the impact of the Treaty of Versailles after World War I. There are even more aspects to the topic that students need to understand to be able to properly address the interest question, and our job as educators is to push our gifted students to make these deeper connections.

Just because a topic diverges does not mean it is not part of the same road, and one of our goals as teachers of gifted students should be to help them stay connected to that road. When I've described my role as a teacher of gifted students, I've often equated it to being a herding dog. The students are all moving on their path, and my job is to run around, nipping at their heels, making sure they do not veer too far off the path we need them to get back to.

This is just one example of how we can differentiate using interest, but the process described is one I have used for years. Ultimately, this strategy does depend on a topic we talked about in Chapter 1, which is listening to and valuing what our students love.

As you read this description, some of you might be thinking, "Wait … so I need to tie dinosaurs into every one of my lessons?" Before you throw this book away, the short answer is absolutely no. First, that would be exhausting. Any sort of extension like this requires time and planning, and since we are diverging from the standard curriculum, we need to make sure we are on top of any changes and can justify their inclusion in terms of differentiation, depth, complexity, and expansion of the content. Second, any connections we make for students should feel authentic and meaningful. Gifted students are savvy and can tell when somebody is being inauthentic (Cross, 2021). This stands for our lessons as well. If we present a lesson that is supposed to engage with what they are interested in and the connection is weak and we have no buy-in, they will call us out on it. I have had many lessons where the students have said, "I see what you did there." (Note: this exact phrase has been used by several of my students and is not just a general statement.)

Integrating dinosaurs or whatever students are interested in for differentiation should be meaningful and special. We want to reserve it for when it is going to be most impactful or when our students really need it.

Another consideration with differentiating using interest is that we can empower our students to make these connections for us. By demonstrating early in the school year the ways in which we can build connections between topics and then encouraging students to make their own, we empower them beyond our classroom. I once had some of my gifted students rush up to me on a field trip because they wanted to explain to me how the different colors of lightsabers in *Star Wars* were reflective of motivations in the Cold War. I was not expecting that sort of response during the outing, but I could not help but beam with pride as they were so excited to talk about history.

Summary

Differentiation requires time, consideration for the needs of your students, and understanding of your content. While it is easy to assume that differentiation means more work, I think a better way of describing differentiation is different work. We need to think about our curriculum not just in terms of what the state or nation prescribes, but rather, in terms of our students and how they will access it. In Chapter 5, we discussed the core elements of differentiation, and here we addressed strategies to implement differentiation for gifted students with direct reference to the middle school setting. By considering the readiness, the learning profile, and the interests of our gifted students, we can create a dynamic environment in our classes.

The next chapter will be a bit different, as it will focus on two different lesson plan examples that demonstrate differentiation for gifted students. Throughout the lessons, I will provide commentary about why certain aspects were selected, the ways in which components meet the needs of gifted students, and how the lesson fits in the middle school setting.

Reflection

1. Look at a lesson you've recently taught and consider the ways you worked to meet the needs of all students. Was differentiation present? Did you differentiate considering student readiness, their learning profiles, or student interest? How do you know all students mastered the material?

References

Cash, R. M. (2017). *Advancing differentiation: Thinking and learning for the 21st century* (2nd ed.). Free Spirit Publishing.

Cross, T. L. (2021). Social and emotional development: The role of authenticity in the psychosocial development of students with gifts and talents.

Gifted Child Today, *44*(2), 111–114. https://doi.org/10.1177/10762 17520988777

Duffer, M., & Duffer, R. (Creators). (2016). Stranger things [TV series]. Netflix.

LtoJ Consulting Group. (n.d.). What is the history of LtoJ®? Retrieved August 13, 2022, from https://ltojconsulting.com/what-is-the-history-of-ltoj

Tomlinson, C. A. (1999). *The differentiated classroom: Responding to the needs of all learners*. Association for Supervision and Curriculum Development.

Tomlinson, C. A. (2001). *How to differentiate instruction in mixed-ability classrooms* (2nd ed.). Association for Supervision and Curriculum Development.

Tomlinson, C. A., & Allan, S. D. (2000). *Leadership for differentiating schools & classrooms*. Association for Supervision and Curriculum Development.

Watterson, B. (2012). *The complete Calvin and Hobbes: Book two*. Andrews McMeel Publishing, LLC.

Webb, J. T. (Ed.). (2016). *Misdiagnosis and dual diagnoses of gifted children and adults: ADHD, bipolar, OCD, Asperger's, depression, and other disorders* (2nd ed.). Great Potential Press, Inc.

Winebrenner, S., & Brulles, D. (2018). *Teaching gifted kids in today's classroom* (4th ed.). Free Spirit Publishing.

Winebrenner, S., & Brulles, D. (2008). *The cluster grouping handbook: How to challenge gifted students and improve achievement for all*. Free Spirit Publishing.

Lesson Planbook Commentary

I am a sucker for DVD commentary. There is just something about hearing creative and logistical insights that I find so interesting, but when that is layered over the actual finished product, it is something special. Hearing writers like B.J. Novak and Mindy Kaling from *The Office* share their process and why certain decisions were made can make the final product even more fascinating. As a creator, I always thought understanding the mindset of those creating, beyond static facts, would help guide my own creations.

For this chapter, my goal is to embody the spirit of DVD commentary by presenting two differentiated projects with my thoughts and commentary running along the side. My goal is for you to see the elements of differentiation in action to get a feeling for how you could differentiate your content for gifted learners. In addition, both projects are ones I have personally implemented, with the second being a project an entire grade level participated in. While there is no perfect solution, my hope is that you will find inspiration in these lessons for how you can differentiate for your gifted learners.

All Quiet on the Western Brunch

The following project is one that I did with several 7th grade gifted self-contained classes. Although the whole class itself was comprised of gifted students, there was still differentiation that happened.

DOI: 10.4324/9781003332015-8

Lesson Plan	Commentary
Background:	The first element of differentiation present is content through the choice of novel. *All Quiet on the Western Front* was part of the district's 11th grade reading list, but special permission was granted for the students in my class to read this book as not only did it match the content, but it also provided the level of complexity gifted students need.
This was a culminating activity for a study of the 1929 novel by Erich Maria Remarque, *All Quiet on the Western Front*. The class was a part of a specialized self-contained gifted program, where I taught students literature and history in a block schedule. This unit coincided with a history unit on World War I.	

With any sort of acceleration like this, it is very important to obtain approval at a school and district level. District scope sequences are important things, and teachers at different schools and grade levels make decisions based on an understanding that certain material is covered at certain times. This is not to discourage you from accelerating or making appropriate curricular choices for your students, but rather, to ensure you engage and collaborate with more stakeholders. By working with the teachers and leaders at the high schools your gifted students might attend, you help to open a meaningful conversation that can result in awareness and support outside of your class.

Lesson Plan	Commentary
Curricular Goals: History – students will be able to: • understand the key events of World War I from the German perspective • understand the perspective of soldiers serving in World War I Literature – students will be able to: • track the development of main and minor characters throughout a novel • utilize effective language to create rich descriptions	The history objectives for this project also represent differentiation, as they provide higher-order variations of grade-level standards. At the time I wrote this project, 7th grade students needed to understand the causes and outcomes of World War I. For my gifted students, this objective, while important, did not provide the level of complexity they needed, so additional aspects were presented. Since most of the materials we used were from an English or U.S. perspective, by emphasizing students' understanding of the German perspective, this added to the complexity of what students were learning. In addition, most of history takes a disconnected perspective, focusing on leaders and the actions of the countries; by shifting focus to the soldiers' perspectives, it also served to enrich the understanding of curriculum. None of these extensions to the curriculum detracted from my students mastering the grade-level standards, but rather, meant they had a deeper level of understanding.

Lesson Plan	Commentary
	One other element that needs to be considered is the content integration represented through this project. While this was an English activity, students were reinforcing their understanding of the history curriculum. There is research addressing the value of content integration in supporting gifted students, as seen in models like VanTassel-Baska's Integrated Curriculum Model. By bridging the gap between multiple content areas, this serves to support gifted students' curiosity, as well as allowing them to make further connections with the content (VanTassel-Baska & Wood, 2010).
Materials: • *All Quiet on the Western Front* text • Computer/Chromebook • Access to Google Suite (Google Docs, Google Sites, etc.) • Examples of vivid food descriptions (Food critic/Yelp reviews and clips from *Diners, Drive-ins, and Dives* [Fieri et al., 2007])	The program I taught had ubiquitous technology as a foundation of its design. To open the opportunities for students to research beyond the curriculum and access materials through a variety of sources, access to technology was important. Although computer access has become more widely available, it is still not something every student has, whether in the classroom or at home. Since this activity is so connected to the source text, access to technology was not a requirement. Students could hand write their responses, or if a computer lab/Chromebook cart could only be checked out for a short period time, that was

Lesson Plan	Commentary
	fine. I have never been a fan of technology for technology's sake, and I feel students get a lot more out of activities that have meaning placed behind the technology.
Project Description: As a culmination to reading the novel *All Quiet on the Western Front*, students will work to gain a deeper understanding of the characters within the novel. To do this, students will create a themed menu for a restaurant, where each dish represents one of the six core characters. Students should write their food descriptions in a way that describes the dish while also being representative of the character.	This project was inspired by one my sophomore honors English teacher had us complete. The foundation of this activity is somewhat strange, but the nature of this activity is part of what makes it appealing for working with gifted students. At the core, analogous thinking is a complex skill, and this helps develop those ideas. In addition, for some students, this will push them outside of their comfort zone, requiring them to think outside the box. There is a level of risk associated with these ideas that gifted students might struggle with, so it is important to anticipate the role we play in guiding them through this activity. That struggle is part of what we are looking for as we help gifted students grow. A final component to consider is that the analogous comparisons for character descriptions do not have to be food (when my sophomore English teacher gave us this activity, we could choose anything to base our character descriptions on), but I feel that

Lesson Plan	Commentary
	food is one of the strongest places to start. Since every culture has their own food, this is a topic any student can relate to, so there are opportunities for students to access their backgrounds in the creation of this project.
Introduction:	This introduction works to engage students with the activity while also serving as a formative pre-test. While this lesson would be supported with previous descriptive writing activities, by collecting the student warm-ups, you are able to identify students who will need assistance in writing their descriptions.
Begin by asking students to consider their favorite food (this could have been the attendance question for the day) and have them write a brief description of that food. Tell students that the goal of this description should be for the reader to want to eat that food and encourage students to use sensory words. Once students have written their descriptions, have them share their responses with a partner. If time allows, have two or three students share their responses with the class.	
After this initial activity, ask students what was easy about describing their favorite food, as well as what was difficult. Then explain to students that they are going to take a moment to see how a professional describes food in a way that makes audiences want to travel across the country to get these dishes.	Utilizing the clip from *Diners, Drive-ins, and Dives* further extends this introduction by giving students an example of how experts go about describing food in colorful ways. Not only does this clip engage students, but it also helps provide real-world contextualization for the skills they are being taught.
Show students a clip from Food Network's *Diners, Drive-ins, and Dives*, where host Guy Fieri travels to different local restaurants to try some of their most famous dishes. As students watch, ask them how Guy Fieri makes audiences want to eat each dish?	Another note about using the Guy Fieri clip is that he is a figure who might not connect with middle school students. *Diners, Drive-ins, and Dives* premiered in 2007, so the relevance to younger viewers might not be present. There are other sources which provide vivid

Lesson Plan	Commentary
Explain to students that this activity served as an introduction to their final project: All Quiet on the Western Brunch	descriptions of food that might connect more with middle school students. YouTube and TikTok are filled with content creators doing food reviews that students might already be aware of. One thing to consider, however, is that while a clip from one of these creators might be school appropriate, you need to know their brand well before incorporating it into your classroom.
Activity: Begin by passing out/sharing the project description with students, reviewing the parameters of the assignment with them. This project description should include the following components: 1. Introduction to the project 2. Description of what students will be doing during the project 3. An example of what is expected from students (preferably from a different work the students have read) 4. A description of all the elements students will submit at the end of the project 5. A timeline for when each element should be completed 6. The rubric	When I introduce projects, I tend to over communicate with the class to make sure students fully know what to expect. This includes a complete write-up of the assignment broken into several steps, as well as an oral description. If a student is absent, this write-up really helps to make sure they know what to expect, and, for our students who struggle processing multistep directions or cannot take in all the information at once, helps to provide a foundation to check what they need to complete. For gifted students who like to know all aspects of project before beginning, this also helps to frame the entire task ahead of time.

Lesson Plan	Commentary

It is very important to spend time explaining the rubric to students. While it might all be written out, we cannot assume students understand exactly how we will be grading. Take the time to review each section, helping to highlight what each level on the rubric means. After this introduction, be sure to take time to answer student questions.

Once questions are answered, give students time to work on the project. To do this, establish what active engagement during this time looks like. While each classroom is different, typically, I will explain in words of this sort:

> "During this time, you are expected to be actively working on your Western Brunch project. Active engagement means you are either reviewing samples I shared of food descriptions, researching and finding evidence of characters in the text, or writing your food descriptions. You are welcome to move around the classroom, but please make sure you are making choices that will help you stay on task."

By establishing those expectations, students know what they should do during unstructured time, and this helps make redirections more meaningful.

The rubric is a crucial component to any project, and it is very important that students have it before starting the project. For gifted students with perfectionistic tendencies, not having the basis for how they will be graded can cause a great deal of stress. I have known teachers who preferred not to share rubrics ahead of time with their gifted students, as they felt it resulted in the class working harder and creating better projects. They reasoned that, if students know the minimum required to earn an A, then they will only do the minimum. While I understand this thinking, I do feel it is a dangerous game to play, especially at the middle school level when students can be overwhelmed by expectations. Not even knowing the criteria ahead of time can just make this worse (I share this having been behind on making rubrics and seeing the stress it caused my students).

Lesson Plan	Commentary
While students are working, I move through the class, discussing progress and challenges, celebrating successes, and helping to guide students to complete the project on time. In addition, the introductory activity students completed will help guide them to where my student feedback initially starts. As I meet with each student, my check-ins with them should act as ongoing formative assessments, leading me to support them through guided lessons or any other help they might need.	If there is a concern with quality or the amount of work gifted students will complete, the conferencing time is the perfect place to continue to push students in their thinking. If a student is not reaching the depth or complexity we know they are capable of, this is the opportunity to get them thinking in this way. We do want to be careful, however, of simply asking them to do more just for the sake of doing more. Remember, differentiation is not repeating the same skill over and over after mastery; it is providing depth and complexity beyond grade-level standards.
Closure:	Celebrating student work is one of my favorite things as a teacher, but it is an easy component to forget. When students put so much of their time into working on a project, these celebrations become an opportunity to add closure and help them see the value of what they did.
After students have completed their projects, it is valuable to have a showcase of student work. This can be done using a gallery walk, small-group sharing, or having students share their favorite descriptions in front of the class.	
After students have completed the activity, have them think about their own learning, and debrief the whole class about how they have grown in the specific skills and in what areas they need additional support. For these reflections, I will often use these two questions as exit-tickets where students submit their responses before leaving class. While the project itself serves as a summative assessment, hearing students' own perspectives allows	These student work showcases are also an opportunity to work with students on giving and receiving peer feedback. This is an incredibly powerful skill to learn, and it is one that often needs to be explicitly taught. There is a strong opportunity for a mini lesson, where you review with your students what effective feedback looks like, as well as

Lesson Plan	Commentary

me to gain a better understanding of their perception of their own strengths and weaknesses. In addition, student feedback helps guide future lessons and activities to address the challenges the students see within their work.

how to present feedback and not bombard somebody with negativity. As students learn this skill, it can be helpful to have them write their feedback and submit it to you, where you can meet with them and help adjust their wording to be more effective. While this is something else for you to do, it can pay dividends as students become more effective at giving each other meaningful and valuable feedback.

Elements of Differentiation:

- Content – the content for this lesson is differentiated through the level of complexity students are expected to reach throughout the project. Students are working at the "Create" and "Analyze" levels of Bloom's Taxonomy.

Students also have choice within the activity. They are not limited to the same type of food or even the same characters (there were some characters whom students had to address in the project, while having the freedom to choose the rest). This freedom allows students to demonstrate their understanding without feeling constrained.

- Process – students are working independently throughout this project, but there are still opportunities for collaboration and sharing ideas with each other. This is important, as gifted students learn in a variety of ways. In addition, there is flexibility regarding how students work on the project. Students will start this project in a variety of ways, with some

The elements of differentiation for this activity are closely tied to all aspects. One of the biggest components of this activity that needs to be addressed further is the role of teacher feedback, as this can influence differentiation beyond this project.

As a teacher, I have always let my students drive the learning of the class. Even when I taught special education resource, my goal was to empower my students, and I still employed this same strategy. In both settings, this allowed for individualized feedback and an opportunity to provide additional support or push students farther in their thinking. This is especially meaningful in a class where you have a variety of student ability levels, and you can guide support to address those various levels.

Lesson Plan	Commentary

students diving into writing menu dishes, some researching the type of food they would like to create and aligning dishes with characters, and some analyzing clips and reviews to understand how to tackle this type of writing. The important thing with this element of differentiation is that there is flexibility.

- Process – students are working independently throughout this project, but there are still opportunities for collaboration and sharing ideas with each other. This is important, as gifted students learn in a variety of ways. In addition, there is flexibility regarding how students work on the project. Students will start this project in a variety of ways, with some students diving into writing menu dishes, some researching the type of food they would like to create and aligning dishes with characters, and some analyzing clips and reviews to understand how to tackle this type of writing. The important thing with this element of differentiation is that there is flexibility.
- Learning environment – the learning environment I had for this project was very relaxed, as students were free to sit where they liked, to work quietly alone or with peers, and were encouraged to explore. In this environment, though, there are two key elements I made sure were addressed: respect for different learning needs and my role as teacher.

Lesson Plan	Commentary

Different students have different needs, and explicit attempts to honor these needs are crucial. For students who get value out of discussions with peers, I wanted to make sure they had a space where this could be done. There are also students who require quiet to work effectively. Having these two types of students in the same class can be challenging, but this can be supported by establishing clear expectations. Noting that conversations could happen quietly with redirections if the volume gets too loud is one way. Another is to allow students who need to talk the opportunity to work outside. What is important is that students feel comfortable in the environment, and know that their needs are being addressed. Before any extended work time, I always establish expectations for the class on what active learning looks like and will give redirections if students diverge too far from the expectations.

Another aspect of the learning environment is my role as the teacher. Throughout this process, I am constantly moving around the class, checking in with students, giving feedback, asking questions, and reinforcing what they are doing. Throughout open work time, this is an opportunity to provide focused support for students and allow for even more differentiation to happen. The key is to know and understand where each student is in terms of the content and to be deliberate with these interactions. The teacher's role in a differentiated classroom is not to sit at their desk grading papers or simply asking students, "Are you good?"

Lesson Plan	Commentary
The teacher is active in the learning process with students, noting that each one needs something different.	
• Assessment – the finished menu of character dishes is the basis for the final assessment for this project, and this is graded against an already established rubric. For this project, the rubric would focus more directly on skills rather than content.	
By sharing the grading metrics with students ahead of time, it helps to alleviate stress and concern, as students know how they are being graded. In addition, knowing the metrics up front can allow students to be more creative, as they do not have to question whether what they are doing meets the criteria of the project.	

This project is one that had several iterations throughout my time teaching, but the base activity has always stayed the same. It is an activity that has been challenging to students, and when I consider the skills I want them to be able to demonstrate, they walked away with a much deeper understanding of who each character is.

Museum Day

The next project is one in which all the 8th grade English and history teachers at my school participated; it became a showcase event. Since every 8th grader at the school was participating, I thought this was a great project to showcase how students can be working on the same objectives while extending their learning beyond the standards. In addition, this project also showcases heavy content integration and utilizing student interest as a foundation for differentiation.

Lesson Plan	Commentary
Background:	This was an incredible event for our
The Museum Day project was a collaboration between 8th grade English and history teachers to give students an enriched understanding of World War II content while also practicing and applying research skills. The project concluded with a showcase of student work that was open to the community.	school, and one that I cannot really take credit for creating. While I did differentiate elements for my students, the idea for and development of this project was fully that of the 8th grade team at Sunrise Middle School, Scottsdale, Arizona.
Curricular Goals:	While the Western Brunch activity
History – students will be able to:	had elements of content integration,
• understand elements of World War II from the perspective of either an Ally or Axis country	it was an English activity. This project, however, represents full collaboration between the two
• research a specific topic of their choice in relation to their country	content areas.
English – students will be able to:	This activity could be expanded even further, to include nearly every
• apply research skills by evaluating sources for validity and reliability	subject area. While this would create an even more dynamic event
• create a works cited page in MLA format	for the school, it would also put a pressure on scheduling. As you look to expand participation, set clear goals for what each participant is responsible for.
Materials:	Being a research activity, access to
• Computers/Chromebooks	computers was very important,
• History textbooks	especially since one of the elements
• General craft materials (pens, markers, construction paper, etc.)	was for students to develop skills in assessing validity and reliability.
• Trifold boards	However, there is still value in using more traditional research methods like finding books in the library. My teaching partner at the time had our students use the library for research as part of this activity, and they were

Lesson Plan	Commentary
	astounded by how much valuable information they were able to find in books. While they always had access to a laptop or Chromebook, they did not typically use the library, and adjusting our expectations to support them in growing in this skill was very powerful.

Project Description:

Every 8th grade history class divided their students into one of six countries (United States, Great Britain, France, Germany, Russia, and Japan), and within those groups, students identified a topic about their country during World War II that they wanted to research.

Throughout the weeks leading up to the final showcase, students researched and worked on their final project in both English and history class. Students were researching to create a predesignated number of artifacts that reinforced what they had researched. Groups also had to create a trifold display with information from each topic researched about their country.

The entire school met in the library for students to showcase their artifacts and share what they had learned.

Tapping into student interests is one of the most powerful things we can do as teachers, and it is a strategy used in differentiation for gifted, special education, and English language learners. Through the structure of this project, students were empowered in letting their interests really drive their research and touching on topics that might not get addressed at the level of detail they would like in class.

Another component of this project that was so effective was the way student grades were determined. While students worked in groupings based on their country, they were responsible for individual components of the final display. Even though the group needed to have a trifold, students were not graded as an entire group. This is especially valuable for gifted students who tend not to enjoy group work (Winebrenner & Brulles, 2018).

In talking with many gifted students about this, they feel the concept is unfair, as every member gets the same grade. What they say this means is that one or two of them end up doing all

Lesson Plan	Commentary
	the work, yet everybody, regardless of how much they did, will still get the same final score. By having discrete elements that each member is responsible for, it removes some of the pressure from the group element as well as relieving stress.
Introduction:	The introduction to this activity is very similar to the introduction for the Western Brunch activity. One element that needs to be emphasized with this phase is the discussion of the timeline.
To introduce this activity, brainstorm elements of World War II that students want to learn more about but have not covered. This should be prominently displayed for the class and remain on the board during the description of the activity.	Big projects like these can be difficult for gifted students to manage, as there are a lot of moving parts. An element of asynchronous development is poor executive functioning (Webb, 2016), and it is something for which we need to prepare. This can make the project incredibly difficult for students who struggle with this issue. In addition, since participants are focusing on their interests for this project, it is very easy for them to get lost down rabbit holes as they research. Having a clear description of where they should be in terms of progress is of vital importance for a project like this.
Review with students the guiding document for the project. The project description should include:	
1. Introduction to the project	
2. Description of what students will be doing during the project	
3. An example of what is expected from students (preferably from previous student projects)	
4. A description of all the elements students will submit at the end of the project	
5. A timeline for when each element should be completed	To help my gifted students manage their time, I utilize what I call soft and hard deadlines. A soft deadline describes an ideal place a student should be with completing a specific task. If a student is not finished with a component when a soft deadline is due, there is no penalty, but rather, at this time they should evaluate their pace or plan. Hard deadlines describe final due
6. The rubric	
Review any questions students might have.	

Lesson Plan	Commentary
	dates for components that students need to have completed. These include the final due date for a project, but I also include other major checkpoints using hard deadlines. If students are behind on their hard deadlines, this then becomes a conference where the two of us must develop a plan for completing the assignment.
Activity: During class, students are actively working on their projects. This includes research and creation of the artifacts they will display. What is important to note with this activity is that students will be working in both English and history class, so those teachers will need to clearly communicate to make sure students receive enough dedicated class time. This collaboration also allows students to complete the project at school without losing all instructional time to work. When students are doing the project in English, they might be doing an activity in history or vice versa. The important thing is that there is collaboration between all teachers involved.	The teacher feedback process is especially important during this time, and differentiation based on student readiness can occur. While students are researching, for example, students who need more support in accessing the curriculum can be provided with resources that will help them better understand the content; while students who have shown mastery can find higher-order resources that challenge their thinking. What is beautiful about this is that since students are choosing their topics, it allows for very individualized resources to be cultivated. In addition, since students are letting their interests guide their research, there are opportunities for students who might struggle at other times to shine. As teachers, we must constantly be assessing our students' progress and adjusting appropriately.

Lesson Plan	Commentary
Closure:	The final Museum Day presentations
The day before the final library showcase, all students set up their displays in the library, organizing materials and preparing their elevator pitch explanations about their resources.	are incredibly hectic but a wonderful showcase of student learning. Parents visit to see the displays, and students beam with pride over the work they have created. It is truly a wonderful day!
During the Museum Day presentation, the entire school comes out to see the displays and talk to students. Throughout the day, the English and history teachers assess the students based on the rubrics for each class.	With the grading, it is important to make sure there is clarity and equity in the ways students are graded between the subjects. For a class like English, I remember many frustrated students who had major deductions because they were missing a works cited page while they got full credit in history. While the two subjects are assessing different skills and content, it is important not to make one teacher the "bad guy." Find a way to create rubrics that will be fair and effective in their assessment while not putting all the pressure on one content area.
Elements of Differentiation:	One of the biggest considerations
• Content – student interest was the driving force of differentiation for this lesson. Since students were able to choose their topic, there was an added level of depth and complexity that closely aligns with Tomlinson's differentiation strategies (Tomlinson, 2001).	about the elements of differentiation for this project was adjusting the project parameters to provide my gifted students with more depth and complexity. The creation of the museum artifacts was an effective way to check student understanding of
I also added an additional element of differentiation for my students. As part of their group write-ups, I also had the groups evaluate the economic, political, and geographic impact of World War II on their countries. This added layer moved the students to consider the larger implications of the war on their country, while also adding the evaluative element of Bloom's Taxonomy to the mix.	their research, but for gifted students, this element was not particularly challenging. During my time meeting with students, an emphasis was placed on the larger impact of these individual research components, asking students to also bridge that gap to the economic, political, and geographic aspects.

Lesson Plan	Commentary

- Process – with the adjustment to the content component, students were working independently and collaboratively. These additional conversations were valuable in differentiating the content for the class, and really emphasized having the students consider the ways in which each of their separate elements coalesced to impact their country. This flexibility in the process also contributed to supporting students' individual learning profiles (Tomlinson, 2001).
- Learning environment – the learning environment for this project was very fluid, and no two students were working on the same topic. This meant a great amount of individualization, while also supporting students exploring their interests. The added layer of collaboration also helped reinforce meaningful student discussions, as students were able to draw off the experiences of their peers' research.
- Assessment – the final assessment for this project shifted the focus for the language component away from citing sources. As part of the natural curriculum my teaching partner and I created, students were citing their sources in MLA format throughout their 7th grade experiences, so we emphasized the evaluation of sources. For the history component, students demonstrated mastery regarding their understanding of how their specific research component impacted their country during World War II.

This project was one that required specific differentiation to support gifted students in meeting their academic needs. In considering projects like this, looking to Bloom's Taxonomy is an important aspect in making sure that gifted students' academic needs are being met. Even a slight variation on what is expected can extend the assignment for students and help them consider the content in much deeper ways.

Summary

This chapter presented two differentiated projects with commentary discussing the choices and perspectives regarding their implementation for gifted learners. The strategies housed within each project can be applied to a variety of subjects, and it is important we consider the lessons learned in these projects as we develop ways to help our students explore the curriculum.

Reflection

1. Look at a recent project you have given to your class. How do students who have demonstrated mastery approach this project? How do students who have not yet demonstrated mastery approach the same project? What changes could you make that would help all learners to have their unique academic needs met?

References

Fieri, G. et al. (Executive Producers). (2007). *Diners, drive-ins, and dives* [TV series]. Food Network.

Tomlinson, C. A. (2001). *How to differentiate instruction in mixed-ability classrooms* (2nd ed.). Association for Supervision and Curriculum Development.

VanTassel-Baska, J., & Wood, S. (2010). The Integrated Curriculum Model (ICM). *Learning and Individual Differences, 20*(4), 345–357. https://doi.org/10.1016/j.lindif.2009.12.006

Webb, J. T. (Ed.). (2016). *Misdiagnosis and dual diagnoses of gifted children and adults: ADHD, bipolar, OCD, Asperger's, depression, and other disorders* (2nd ed.). Great Potential Press, Inc.

Winebrenner, S., & Brulles, D. (2018). *Teaching gifted kids in today's classroom* (4th ed.). Free Spirit Publishing.

What's in a Grade?

In a 2014 episode of the ABC sitcom *Modern Family*, a main character, Claire, attends her daughter's high school's open house. In each of the Advanced Placement classes, the teachers discuss the importance of the end-of-the-year assessment, the amount of homework parents should expect their children to complete each night, as well as different practice exams students should complete before the actual test. When one of the teachers proudly proclaims that she "only" assigns two hours of homework each night, Claire cannot believe how much is being asked of each student. She adds up the different hourly estimates from each period, realizing that, just between four of her daughter's classes, there is an expectation of six hours of homework a night (Bagdonas, 2014).

While the scenario from *Modern Family* is set in a high school, this is a reality many of our gifted middle schoolers face. They are being pulled in so many directions, often by the adults around them, and they must figure out how to manage it all. What makes this even more difficult is that this time coincides with some of the last moments of childhood they will have. As educators, we have a great deal of power in helping them enjoy a few more minutes of this precious time.

Beyond the Classroom

Think about the typical day for one of your gifted students. If we assume school starts at 8:00 am and ends at 2:30 pm, that means there are approximately seven and a half hours left in the day. If that student is involved in an

DOI: 10.4324/9781003332015-9

extracurricular activity after school, let's say that ends at 4:00 pm, meaning the student now has six hours left in their day. If it takes 30 minutes to travel home, that student now has five and a half hours left in their day. That is it.

Five and a half hours to eat, do homework, socialize with friends, spend time with family, and have the chance to do something they find valuable. While the *Modern Family* example was set in a high school, if we divide the homework expectation in half, that is three hours dedicated to working outside of the school day. The estimate assumes that the child completes the homework in the time frame the teacher expects and does not require any additional support. It assumes the child does not have any other responsibilities, like helping with dinner or watching younger siblings.

The estimate assumes that school is the only thing in the lives of our students.

The reality is that our gifted middle schoolers have responsibilities and interests that extend far beyond the walls of our classrooms, and while what we do is important, it is not the only thing. There are several external and internal stressors gifted students are dealing with, and we need to be aware that those factors weigh heavily on them. Gifted children tend to have an awareness of the world, picking up on the subtle cues they see, and worrying about how they can help (Clark, 2002). I have seen this happen with my students with big, overarching topics like climate change or the COVID-19 pandemic. As the world felt like it was spiraling out of control, they took that stress on, trying to figure out how they could make a difference when the problem was so overwhelming.

These personal stressors can also reflect aspects of their own lives, as they worry about how they will get to school or family finances. We have many gifted students from low socioeconomic environments who have to take on even more of this stress, as parents work and they need to care for younger siblings. As we consider that five and a half hours students have after school, we need to understand that, for some, that time is filled with being a babysitter, all before they can even think about themselves.

On the other side, we have students whose lives are filled to the brim with extracurricular activities, as the pressure to get into a good college or continue with a lifelong passion puts added stress on them. No longer is high school the place where stellar athletes are discovered, as scouts now look at club sports to find young talent (NCSA, n.d.). When I coached middle school sports, many of my students from class participated, so I got to see them in a very different light. I saw how busy their lives were, as they would leave my practice at 4:00 pm to head to their club team practice until 7:30 pm or 8:00 pm.

One of the most brilliant students I ever had was an Olympic-caliber gymnast. They competed nationally and were a genuine contender for the Games. The level they were competing at required a significant investment in time. Their family coordinated with the administration so that they would leave school early to practice at the gym for around six hours every day. This meant doing homework and eating in the car on the way there. While that is an extreme example, I have had many gifted middle school students share with me their experience of not getting home until right before bed.

The lives of our gifted middle schoolers are incredibly busy for a variety of reasons. Whether it is scheduling, survival, or an inability to start because of the weight of the world, there are factors outside of our classroom impacting the lives of our students. While we can't change the world, we can change our classrooms to make *their* worlds just a little more manageable.

Does Anybody Like Grading Homework?

As I have grown, I have learned a lot of hard lessons that only come with experience. While the significance of these lessons ranges from minor (seeing *Batman v Superman* a third time does not make it a better movie) to more important (it's a good idea to make sure there are actually diapers in the diaper bag), there is one lesson that hit hard in my first year of teaching: if you assign homework, you have to grade it all in a timely manner.

This seems obvious, but, being an English teacher, I severely underestimated the amount of time it would take not just to read through every assignment, but also provide valuable feedback for my students. If a student wrote an incorrect response, I needed to make sure I explained why their response was incorrect; on the other end, I wanted to make sure that students understood what they did well on an assignment, so that also meant providing feedback on correct responses, sometimes highlighting areas where they could provide more depth. In my first year teaching the gifted self-contained class, I had 60 students, and if it took me five minutes to grade each individual assignment, that meant a total of 300 minutes per assignment, or five hours. This amount of time is significant, and the funny thing about classwork is that curriculum continues to move on regardless of whether we want it to or not.

As I think about homework, I cannot help but wonder: why do we assign so much?

I know this is a delicate topic for many teachers, and there are many different philosophies surrounding homework implementation. I have spoken with math teachers who explained the importance of iterative practice when it comes to mastering content, and I completely understand and agree with this perspective. There are elements of homework that are incredibly valuable, but simply adding more work does not yield higher benefits.

A 2015 study from Spain considering the effectiveness of homework on adolescent students identified the ideal duration for homework as one hour per night (Fernández-Alonso et al., 2015). While the authors note there is still a benefit to homework, they also emphasized that the quality and consistency of the homework were important considerations (Fernández-Alonso et al., 2015).

Another study, which sampled 4,317 students, had an average homework load of three hours per night (Galloway et al., 2013). Through a mixture of quantitative and qualitative data, the authors found that more time spent on homework resulted in increased stress, impacts to health, and less time for friends, family, and extracurricular activities (Galloway et al., 2013). In addition, while they acknowledged that students were more engaged with school the more time they spent working, Galloway et al. explained that this engagement did not reflect depth of learning, with many students even noting that the work had little value (2013).

There is also the reality of how homework is graded. I will be the first to admit that I have fallen into this trap – there are times when I have homework assignments students have submitted that do not get returned for weeks. That means that when students eventually get the work back with my feedback, we have moved on to new topics, so the feedback the students received does not help to guide them in their understanding or mastery of the current subject. If we think about the breakdown of a student's day, any work we ask them to complete outside of class has a significant impact on their time, so the value needs to be apparent. What's more, though, is the message we communicate to our students with homework and the feedback we provide. If we are not acting on the homework we assign students, we are essentially saying we do not value their time.

The other critical component we need to understand when considering homework is the role this plays with gifted students. Just as with differentiation, the number of repetitions a gifted student needs to demonstrate mastery is less than for age-level peers (Winebrenner & Brulles, 2018), meaning that as we assign homework, if it is simply being done for the iterative practice, our gifted students require less. In fact, Fernández-Alonso et al. advise against having homework centered on "repetition or revision of content" (2015, p. 1083). The challenges gifted students experience with homework are complex, and assigning work they do not find value in can result in resentment, frustration, or not completing the work at all.

Responsibility versus Ability

When discussing homework, I find it impossible not to talk about grading, as homework tends to be an area that can completely devastate a student's grade. If a student does not turn in a homework assignment, then the natural response is for that student not to receive any credit. As more and more of these missing assignments add up, it can result in a student receiving a failing grade, regardless of what they know about the subject. For every missing assignment, that student receives a zero in the grade book.

In many ways it reminds me of the climax of the film *Willy Wonka & the Chocolate Factory*. After touring Wonka's factory, making it through all the different pitfalls the other ticket recipients fell into, Charlie and his grandfather think they are about to win an amazing prize, only to be told that they were disqualified for stealing fizzy-lifting drinks. Wonka screams at the two, "You get nothing! You lose! Good day, sir" (Stuart, 1971). When we have students who do not turn in work and we simply put a zero in the grade book, we are essentially telling them that they lose and to have a good day.

While the logic makes sense – they did not do the assignment, so they do not receive the credit, we really must think about what a zero actually means. Dr. Kimberly Lansdowne, curriculum and program designer for gifted students, would explain to her staff that by placing a zero in the grade book, a teacher is essentially saying that this student did not learn a single thing related to that topic (personal communication, n.d.).

Throughout every class period, lecture, and in class activity, the grade book is saying for that standard or objective, this student does not have any content mastery.

When I first heard this explanation, it was a valuable shift in understanding for me. I had always worked with my students to allow them to make up assignments or turn in late work for credit, but hearing Lansdowne's explanation helped me to reconsider what the grade book means. It should reflect how students are progressing in their understanding and mastery of the curriculum objectives you are using. With each assignment, you should be able to identify the skills and/or the content mastery students are demonstrating through the completion of the task.

I can remember early in my career having a meeting with a gifted middle school student and their parents, discussing why they were struggling in my class. The answer was obvious: they were missing most of the assignments we had done that quarter. As we looked at the grade book more closely and the assignments this student had completed, however, it was clear that they had a strong mastery of the content when they submitted the assignments. The only reason their grade was failing was because they had so much missing work. During the meeting I explained that this grade was not a reflection of their ability, but rather, their sense of responsibility.

While a sense of responsibility is an important trait, is that what a social studies grade book should be reflecting, especially when there is clear evidence that the student understands the content? This meeting led me to reflect a lot on my practice as a teacher and how I was assessing student learning

Double Down

As I researched grading practices and missing assignments specifically, one of the things that really stood out to me was the impact that a zero has on a student's grade. If we think of standard grade distribution, each grade has 10% separating it from the next grade, except for the F. From 59% to 0%, a student will fail an assignment. More than half of the points for any assignment are identifying that a student failed. Because of this structure, that means that a 0 in the grade book is like failing twice.

In an article for Edutopia, Alexis Tamony describes the impact a single 0 can have. She describes a student who scores 85% on every assignment, but has a "missing" for the third assignment. In order to get their grade back to a B, the student would need to earn 85% on 16 assignments (Tamony, 2021). I have seen students get frustrated and feel defeated as they try to complete assignments to fix their grade. This effort, though, can feel like they are trying to scoop water out of a boat with a hole in it.

What is especially important to consider regarding missing assignments and gifted students, is that the sense of responsibility and study skills needed are not always developed by the time they reach middle school. One of the characteristics of asynchronous development is a lack of judgment (Webb, 2016), and these study skills might not have been something they were taught. If gifted students have not been challenged in elementary school, then the typical structure of learning how to allocate time and study is not there. By not learning how to apply these skills, they are entering middle school at a disadvantage.

Does that mean we should not hold our gifted students accountable? Absolutely not! We have a responsibility to our students, their future teachers, and ourselves to equip them with the skills necessary to be successful. What we need, however, is a shift in how we think about homework and our grade books.

What's the Point?

While the discussions of homework and the grade book feel separate, they are very closely related. It is impossible to talk about homework without considering its impact on the grade book and vice versa.

The first consideration that needs to occur with any homework assignment (and really any assignment) is to ask what is the point. Why this assignment? What are you hoping to gain from it and why must it be assigned to do at home? Is this practice of a skill already taught in class or a preview of new content? These are questions I ask myself when I assign homework, and they are things I overtly address with my students. I explain to them the reasoning behind the assignment, what its purpose is, and why I need them to complete it at home. For example, when I assign students end-of-chapter questions from the history text, I will explain to them that having them read through the chapter before we have learned the material acts as a preview to content, which, in turn, allows me to move through at a quicker pace. In addition, I tell them to identify topics they find confusing or want more information on when we come to address the topic in class. Finally, I will explain that the questions they answer help to provide me with a foundation for their understanding of the material, as well as how they are answering the questions. This will then guide future lessons, shaping how we will move forward.

While this seems like a lot of justification to provide, it can be helpful in supporting gifted students in understanding "why are we learning this" and add buy-in to the assignment. Furthermore, this discussion with the students allows for an opportunity to address differentiation, where you can identify the hardest questions first or provide outlets for students who might want to challenge themselves in a different way (Winebrenner & Brulles, 2008).

This transparency also goes a long way in gaining respect from the class, as you are addressing them as adults, essentially pulling the curtain back on the mystery of teaching. As students move into adolescence, this respect helps to foster trust and establish the reciprocation of trust. In addition, one of the potential factors in gifted underachievement rests in the ways students feel about teachers (Sousa, 2009), and getting buy-in for strategies and assignments can help combat this.

In running through these questions before assigning homework, I have severely cut back on what I assign. This will usually mean incorporating questions or topics into in-class activities or realizing they are already addressed elsewhere. In my experience, this has not resulted in any significant difference in learning, and more importantly, when I do assign homework, my students have been more willing to apply themselves, as they know I have considered their time and placed value on it.

Letting Your Students Return the Gobstopper

It is inevitable that at least one of our middle school gifted students will falter at some point in getting work submitted on time. This could be for a variety of reasons, but we always need to remember that our students have a life outside of our classes. While we will have those who missed an assignment because they were playing video games, we will have others who were not able to complete their work because they have the weight of the world on their shoulders – responsibilities that make history or math seem small in comparison.

For all our students, I think it is important to learn from Willy Wonka.

After Wonka told Charlie that he did not get the prize, Charlie's grandfather was upset, and told his grandson they would get revenge by handing over the Everlasting Gobstopper to a rival candy maker. As the two were about to leave, Charlie walked over to Wonka and returned the candy, having promised earlier in the film not to tell a single other soul about it. Upon seeing the Gobstopper, Wonka leaps up, congratulating Charlie on completing the final test (Stuart, 1971).

In my experience, we educators, especially at the secondary level, can easily fall into the trap of prioritizing policies and procedures over our students. While these features outlined in the syllabus are designed to prepare them for the future, these same elements can be devastating to their grades and their self-concept. Zero tolerance policies on late work or 50% deductions for turning in an assignment late might seem like they will motivate students to get their work submitted on time, but this can create the opposite effect, as students either stress over getting assignments completed or are penalized, sometimes for things outside of their control.

While the scene from *Willy Wonka & the Chocolate Factory* was a test for Charlie, the reality is that Charlie was in the wrong. He did violate the contract and should have been disqualified, but he was given the chance to prove his character. How many of our students do not get the chance to prove their knowledge or understanding because of the policies we have in place?

Just like with assigning homework, we need to consider how late and missing assignments impact the students. For gifted adolescents this is incredibly important, as it allows them to see that they can make mistakes, and that we are there to support them. Create policies that still hold students accountable, but just make sure they are designed in a way that allows them to return the gobstopper.

It's Alright to Have Fun

The rest of this chapter will shift the focus away from the technical aspects of teaching to address something critical as teachers of gifted middle school students: we need to be their advocates. Up until this point, this book has identified their academic and social-emotional needs, but we also sometimes need to advocate another important message: it's alright to have fun and be a kid. One of my favorite parts of working with gifted middle schoolers is the wide array of topics you can cover while still having fun; however, there are times when the students and the parents need to be reminded of this.

I am not sure what it is, but I have worked with many gifted students who take themselves and the work they do a bit too seriously. As a former gifted kid who took himself too seriously, I understand this perspective; school is a place where you are supposed to work hard and learn as it will prepare you for your future. While this is true, we do have gifted students who will take their dedication to an extreme. For example, I have had students who got annoyed with others playing basketball at lunchtime because they felt it was a waste of time and activities like sports were pointless. Although these students had activities and hobbies of their own, they tended to be academically focused.

There were also students who had big, yet attainable, goals of attending prestigious schools. Everything they did was part of a well-researched plan to reach their goal, and middle school was a building block in that ultimate tower. The clubs and activities in which they participated were calculated into the equation of what would set them apart from their peers.

In all my years teaching gifted students, it can be hard to distinguish the line between the student's dreams and the parents' dream of supporting their child. Whether intentional or not, there was a great deal of pressure from parents to attain these goals, even if the goal changed. A student once shared with me that, while attending a camp for gifted students, all the kids there basically said their futures were already written. Regardless of their passions or interests, these kids felt they had to enter careers in either medicine, law, or engineering. These students felt trapped in their own potential.

This same pressure is felt by so many of our gifted students, who, even if the goal is not Harvard, still have incredible expectations placed on them because of their gifts and talents. Even in books on guiding gifted learners, sections discussing gifted adolescents transitioning to high school suggest touring colleges to help motivate them to understand what doing well in school could mean. While well intentioned, this approach places an incredible amount of pressure on our gifted teens who are at a critical point in their lives. Couple this with the fact that many gifted students have a strong sense of right and wrong (Clark, 2002); if there are established rules, those rules are not meant to be broken. If parents and teachers are setting expectations that there needs to be a constant vision of the future, then middle school, the last moments of childhood, can be lost without realizing it.

What are we supposed to do? There is pressure on both ends, because while many gifted students have pressure to achieve, there are others to whom school after high school seems like an impossibility. These are students who would be the first of their families to attend college. They might struggle in school or the rising cost of college is prohibitive. One of the foundations of the AVID (Advancement Via Individual Determination) program is for teachers to display memorabilia from the colleges they attended so students have college in their minds and understand that it is attainable. This is such a powerful thing, and something many gifted middle schoolers need.

There is no perfect answer, but finding a balance is key. Have high expectations for your classes. Help them dream and set goals for those dreams. Work together with families and help equip them with resources. Let your students know that you believe in them. However, do not lose sight of the fact that they are still kids. Let them be goofy. Let them laugh. Model for them that even when they work hard, they can still find moments to be kids. The fun attendance questions described in Chapter 2 are a great resource for this, as they provide quick opportunities for students to laugh and let their guard down. We need to communicate balance, and let our students know that we understand there is more to life than what happens inside our classrooms.

This can be very effectively communicated with students through our handling of assigning work over long weekends or extended breaks. While it is best practice not to assign work during these times, I have seen many teachers assign readings or have tests scheduled for immediately after a break. This sends such a negative message to our students and families and places an unnecessary pressure on a time that should be relaxing. Whenever my students have long breaks, my homework assignment is always the same: do something that is just for you. I tell them that they need to relax during breaks, and that they should use that time to do something they might not have time for otherwise. I give examples like binge watching a show, playing a video game, reading a non-school assigned book, doing an art project just for you, or getting outside and playing. I tell students that I will follow up to make sure they did something relaxing over the break (that is usually my attendance question for the first day after a break), and it is always astounding to me to see the excitement in their faces over being told they have permission to be a kid. I have even had students ask that I designate "have fun" as an assignment on our class website so their parents can see they are supposed to relax.

We do not want to be in conflict with parents, but we hold a great deal of power in the culture we set and the ways we look out for our students. During a meet the teacher night, I had a parent of a new gifted 7th grader ask me something surprising. After the natural small talk, they asked if I would encourage their child to stop reading *Captain Underpants* books and start reading more high-quality literature they felt was more appropriate. I respectfully told them that in my English class we would be reading a lot of high-school-level texts that would challenge their child, and I thought it was great they were reading for fun, regardless of the content. I explained that we would be having a lot of in-depth literary discussions, and if *Captain Underpants* was something the student loved, I did not think it should be taken away.

The intentions were good, but taking away something the student loved would not help foster their gifts. I did not know this at the time, but that student was an amazing cartoonist and drew a great deal of inspiration from *Captain Underpants*. Being a cartoonist myself, I loved seeing what they were working on, and many of their cartoons adorned the walls of my classroom. Had they not been given that outlet, I do not know what their middle school experience would have been like, but with it, I know they were able to laugh and be themself.

There is a lot of pressure from the world to grow up, but once you do, there is no going back. If we can create an environment that lets our gifted middle schoolers stay kids for just a little bit longer, I think we owe it to them. Through asynchronous development they are already torn, but we can help them understand that both parts are central to who they are.

Summary

Gifted middle schoolers are faced with a lot of pressures that can impact the limited time they have. Between school, homework, extracurricular activities, and other responsibilities, gifted students can find managing all these elements challenging. By considering the nature of homework and grading policies, the classroom can help support students in finding balance in their lives.

Reflection

1. What do the lives of your gifted students look like outside your classroom? What are their responsibilities? What are the pressures they face?
2. What is something you wish you could be doing right now? Find an opportunity to do it! Take a break from reading this book and do something for yourself.

References

Bagdonas, J. (Director). (2014, January 15). Under Pressure (12, season 5) [TV series episode]. In *Modern Family*. ABC.

Clark, B. (2002). *Growing up gifted* (6th ed.). Merrill Prentice Hall.

Fernández-Alonso, R., Suárez-Álvarez, J., & Muñiz, J. (2015). Adolescents' homework performance in mathematics and science: Personal factors and teaching practices. *Journal of Educational Psychology, 107*(4), 1075–1085. https://doi.org/10.1037/edu0000032

Galloway, M., Conner, J., & Pope, D. (2013). Nonacademic effects of homework in privileged, high-performing high schools. *Journal of Experimental Education, 81*(4), 490–510. https://doi.org/10.1080/00220973.2012.745469

NCSA. (n.d.). High school vs club sports. Retrieved August 27, 2022, from www.ncsasports.org/recruiting/how-to-get-recruited/club-sports

Sousa, D. A. (2009). *How the gifted brain learns* (2nd ed.). Corwin.

Stuart, M. (Director). (1971, June 30). *Willy Wonka & the chocolate factory* [Film]. Paramount Pictures.

Tamony, A. (2021, October 6). The case against zeros in grading. Edutopia. Retrieved from www.edutopia.org/article/case-against-zeros-grading

Webb, J. T. (Ed.). (2016). *Misdiagnosis and dual diagnoses of gifted children and adults: ADHD, bipolar, OCD, Asperger's, depression, and other disorders* (2nd ed.). Great Potential Press, Inc.

Winebrenner, S., & Brulles, D. (2018). *Teaching gifted kids in today's classroom* (4th ed.). Free Spirit Publishing.

Winebrenner, S., & Brulles, D. (2008). *The cluster grouping handbook: How to challenge gifted students and improve achievement for all*. Free Spirit Publishing.

The Need for Mentors

Throughout fiction there are countless examples of mentors who guide heroes on their quests. From Gandalf to Mr. Miyagi, they provide insight that only comes with experience, and even if their methods seem unconventional, there always is a purpose. Probably the most famous of all fictional mentors is Yoda. The master Jedi who first appeared in the 1980 film *The Empire Strikes Back* is well known even to those who do not follow the Star Wars franchise. Quotations like "Do or do not. There is no try" (Kershner, 1980) or "The greatest teacher, failure is" (Johnson, 2017) are not just reserved for a galaxy far, far away, but can be applied to each and every one of our lives.

Our gifted middle schoolers are looking for the same sort of guidance and expertise for the areas they are passionate about. While we can enrich our curriculum and differentiate to engage our students, there is something irreplaceable about the guidance and insights of an external expert. This chapter provides an overview of the value gifted learners receive from mentors, while also describing ways you can collaborate with experts in the field.

The Need for Academic Mentors

One of the hardest things about working with gifted students is realizing that there are going to be many times you are not the smartest person in the room. This will not be true for every subject or every day, but if you work with gifted students long enough, you will likely have a moment where

DOI: 10.4324/9781003332015-10

you go, "They know a lot more about this than I do." For me that happened regularly with science. Although I never taught the subject, I would have conversations with my students about what they were learning, and we would inevitably reach the point where I could not help them or could simply nod my head as they taught me. This would even happen in history, a subject I have taught for more than a decade, where students would correct a detail I shared or add additional information to the discussion that I did not know.

This can be a jolting feeling and a hit to your confidence, but the reality is that nobody expects you to have all the answers. In fact, knowing and understanding this is incredibly important, because it allows you to connect your gifted students with people who can answer their questions and challenge them.

Many gifted education texts speak to the importance of mentorships with gifted students (Clark, 2002; Rogers, 2002; Winebrenner & Brulles, 2018). Through working with an expert within an area of focus, gifted students can grow in their understanding of the material beyond what they can learn within the classroom. In many ways, working with a mentor acts as a form of content acceleration, as students are learning content beyond the established grade-level standards (Rogers, 2002). As Winebrenner and Brulles explains, however, mentorships are not a replacement for gifted services, but act as a supplement (2018). While most programs like this are implemented at the high school level, there is some concern that these programs should start before 9th grade, with researcher Kerry Casey suggesting possibly starting in upper elementary school (Casey, 2000).

For a truly in-depth review of mentorship resources, the Davidson Institute, an organization dedicated to supporting gifted students (Davidson Institute for Talent Development, n.d.), has many materials available to educators and parents regarding mentorships. Specifically, their *Mentoring Guidebook* is valuable for understanding this process (Davidson Institute for Talent Development, 2021).

Challenges in Implementing Mentorships at the Middle School Level

While there is a need to support gifted students with mentors, there are challenges in implementing a mentorship-style program in middle school since students are minors. One of the most important things in any program development is to follow school and district protocols. For example, many districts have requirements that anyone working with students must be fingerprinted and background screened. This is an additional step that can slow down the process, and it is critical we follow these procedures to protect students and not breach district policy. In addition, not following these procedures can have consequences for you, so please make sure you work with your leadership team in advance of launching a new initiative.

A second challenge may be acquiring suitable mentors to work with gifted students. If you do not have immediate connections to experts in various fields, knowing how to identify and kick off these relationships may be difficult. To get started, connect with your staff. Your colleagues have a great wealth of information and letting them know that you are looking for an expert in a specific field can yield great results. These connections are also strong, as there is the additional layer of having a fellow teacher vouch for somebody. This may not clear every problem that might arise, but will help support your efforts in finding quality mentors.

In addition, reaching out to your parent community is also very powerful. Connecting with parents can help develop trust and support between the school and home, and having that relationship is invaluable. If parents know that we trust and value their perspectives and expertise, this can go a long way in working together to support our students. In addition, by reaching out to parents, we might discover expertise that we never knew was there. At my school, as part of enrichment for our students, the principal reached out to the community to find out if parents were available to teach elective-style classes for our students. By reaching out, our school has been fortunate to have a master woodworker and two exceptional artists work with and guide our students. The value from their support cannot be overstated, and it all came from just asking the community.

Another option is to reach out to local community college and university faculty. Connecting with the head of a department can yield great information, as they are aware of the specialties of their departments, as well as who might work well with middle school students. One thing to consider, however, is any relationship the school district might already have with local colleges. If there is an existing dual enrollment program or similar relationship, it is important that any work you do does not disrupt this.

Expert Guests

While the traditional mentorship model might be difficult to implement in a middle school class, that does not mean we lose out on the benefits of working with a mentor. Instead, we must be creative about the enriching and meaningful experience that can come from working with somebody from a specific field. By connecting with experts to support our classes, we can engage students in a deeper understanding of their content, while also helping to forge meaningful professional relationships.

Guest speakers in classrooms are common, but worth noting as they provide a meaningful way for gifted students to connect with experts in the field and explore specific subjects at a deeper level. Since there are many components that go into a formal mentorship, this is an easily implemented way to support quickly connecting gifted students to experts in the field. Through video conferencing software like Zoom or Google Hangouts, working with speakers from all over the country or even the world is easier than ever. As educators, we can research a topic and present clips or videos; however, there is something powerful and significant when hearing from someone directly within the field. Many of my gifted students have always done well at understanding the history content I have taught, but this is nothing compared to the engagement and reflection I have seen when we have had experts join us.

One of the most powerful examples of this I can recall is also one of my most embarrassing teacher stories. When teaching the gifted self-contained middle school program, there were many ridiculous or silly moments that would come up, and a frequent joke I would make would be, "And then the President walks in." The students always found this funny since the ridiculous was always outpaced by meaningful learning, but the thought of the President coming in to see great learning and being met with whatever random discussion we were having was too much.

At the end of the school year, I was introducing a final history research project where the class was broken into groups to research a decade of the Cold War. The students had an entire class period to present on the topic, dress in decade-appropriate clothing, and even teach the class a dance from that time period. When the students learned that they would need to dress in costumes and dance, one of them replied, "Wouldn't it be funny if the President walked in?" As the class laughed, I replied with, "Let's invite him!" They were confused about this, but I explained that citizens can write to elected officials. We went ahead and sent invitations to the President, the mayor, and a senator of their choice. This became a meaningful writing activity and a brief civics lesson.

In support of the class, my teaching team and I all dressed up along with the students. When the 1970s group presented, I too was dressed for the disco. As the group was getting ready to present, there was a knock on the door, and when I opened it, my assistant principal was standing there with the mayor. After my initial shock and embarrassment, we welcomed the mayor to watch the class presentation. He conversed with the students, answering their questions and giving his insights on the history content they were learning. He also explained that he changed his schedule, moving a meeting he had that day in order to attend the class presentation. He joked that when an elected official receives 40 invites from the children of voters, it is in his best interest to honor what they want. The original goal of this history lesson was further amplified, as not only did the class gain a stronger understanding of the content, but the mayor's personal insights provided an even deeper understanding and sense of connection to the larger community.

What is important when incorporating an expert guest into your classroom is that the experience is not passive. Part of the value of having gifted students work with mentors is that they are connected to a source of depth and complexity they are seeking. If students are just passive recipients to a lecture, there is not the same value. When the mayor came to meet with my class, they did not just hear a scripted presentation; they asked questions and were able to share their insights. While we had not formally planned this meeting, the interactions they had were driven by them.

To provide students with this more individualized experience, I highly recommend allowing them to meet with the expert in small groups to get specific questions answered. This will require a larger investment of time (possibly multiple days), but those more focused interactions will bring them closer to the mentor experience. In addition, it is incredibly important that students be prepared in advance with the in-depth, complex questions they have. To do this, dedicating a portion of the class to this before the meeting will allow students to understand what types of questions they should be asking, as well as allowing them to gather any background information they need to support their questions.

This preparation helps ensure that the experience with the expert is valuable, and the limited time they have with the students can be beneficial. If questions are underdeveloped, then gifted students will not get the same benefit. In addition, by spending this time, it places a value on the experience that will increase engagement. Through having well-constructed, higher-order questions, this will foster a meaningful relationship with the expert which, in turn, could lead to return visits or more involved volunteering opportunities. While we want to avoid having an inauthentic dog and pony show for a guest, laying down that foundation can yield incredibly positive results.

In a similar vein, having expert guests lead students in an activity connected to their specific area of focus can help students get hands-on experience and make the curriculum come alive. For example, one year, I was working with a group of accelerated gifted 9th graders, and many of the students were middle school aged. As part of an integrated activity between the humanities and sciences, we worked with a researcher who was conducting a study on tree coverage within city parks. This college professor met with our students and guided them in an activity he had his own college classes do. The students were conducting actual research with an expert in the field. Skills and concepts they learned in class were being applied through this, and while this was not a formal mentorship, the class experienced what it means to be a researcher.

Working in an environment like this is much more involved than just having a guest speaker. Since you will be working with a larger group of students, it is important to understand what the expert guest needs and expects from the class. Background knowledge is one of the biggest components to this, and we want to make sure we are setting our students up for success so they can gain the most they can from the experience. Another factor to consider is if there is a grade associated with the activity and what deliverables are expected. When working with mentors, it is important that they are not the ones grading students, as their role should be to guide (Clark, 2002).

Mentor Programs

One of my goals for this book was to ensure that the examples I provided were based on personal experience. Theory is important; however, I wanted any educator to know that these lessons and strategies were not just conjecture, but things I stood by. That is why, for this section, it is important to note that I have never experienced or seen a formal mentorship program implemented at the middle school level. There are several challenges that come with supporting this age group, and none of the schools I have worked at utilized mentors with 7th and 8th graders. That is not to say that this could not be done, and there is an argument that mentorships should start before high school (Casey, 2000). I have seen these programs be incredibly successful in the upper grades, but they took time and effort to get to that level of success.

If you and your school leadership are considering developing a mentor program at your middle school, I wanted to provide some insights I have gained from observing this program implemented with high school juniors and seniors.

1. *Have clear expectations for the mentor and the mentee.*

   While the idea behind a mentorship seems straightforward, each party involved will have their own idea of what this will look like. It is very important to establish early on what each person's responsibilities are, what the deliverables are, and what will happen if the expectations are not met.

   For students, things like following deadlines and appropriate communication with their mentor are very important components – make sure these are clearly addressed. At no point during the process should students question what is expected of them. Similarly, mentors should understand their responsibility when working with students, as well as what should be produced. It is important to remember that, in many cases, the mentors will not be educators, so some of the nuances of working with adolescents (especially gifted adolescents) will need to be stated.

   For both mentors and mentees, the steps they should take if any responsibilities are not being met should be clearly defined as well. The educator overseeing the mentorship program should be the point of contact for both students and mentors if there are problems, and their goal should be to mediate between the different parties. It should be clear that at the first sign of concern, the advisor should be brought in because this is the easiest time to address any problems.

   At my school, one of the central components of the program is the mentorship handbook. This is the guiding document, and parents, students, and mentors all have access to it. The criteria for participation, student and mentor expectations, as well as the final product are all clearly defined, so there is no question regarding what each party's responsibility is.

2. *Have clearly defined participation criteria.*

A mentorship is a big responsibility, and it is important that there are clearly defined expectations for participation. Since students will be working with members of the community, they will be representing the school, the district, and themselves, so it is important that students are serious about participating.

Having criteria that reference grade point average (GPA) or discipline are important, but it is also critical to remember that gifted students are not always high achieving, so we want to make sure that the application process is not so restrictive that it could remove the students who would benefit greatly from working with a mentor.

Instead of relying solely on GPA, have students complete an application that includes essay-style responses (these could be written or video) where they describe what they hope to gain from the mentorship. This will allow a better understanding of what a student is looking for. From my experience, getting a gifted student talking about their passion will result in them lighting up in a way that might not be seen in the classroom.

It is also important to note that, while the mentorship is designed to support gifted students, you should not exclude students who are not identified as gifted from participating. In fact, the mentorship program could provide a meaningful outlet for students not formally identified as gifted to receive the differentiated support they might be missing elsewhere.

3. *Celebrate student mentorships!*

One of the most important parts of the mentorship experience is the opportunity to share what was accomplished. At the end of the year, my entire school attends our Mentorship Symposium, where all the students who participated in a mentorship get the opportunity to share what they accomplished. Not only does this celebrate the hard work of students participating in a mentorship, but it also allows other students to get excited about the possibility of participating as well. Whatever method works best for your school, be sure to celebrate the hard work of the students!

Summary

Mentorships are regularly recommended as opportunities for gifted students to gain a real-world understanding of content they love at a deeper level. These enriching experiences can be incredibly valuable, but implementation at the middle school level can be difficult. By utilizing experts from various fields in our classes as guest speakers or expert volunteers, this allows students to gain similar benefits to more traditional mentorship programs.

Reflection

1. Think about the members of your community. What opportunities are available for you to integrate their expertise into your class?

References

Casey, K. M. A. (2000). Mentors' contributions to gifted adolescents' affective, social, and vocational development. *Roeper Review, 22*(4), 227. https://doi.org/10.1080/02783190009554043

Clark, B. (2002). *Growing up gifted* (6th ed.). Merrill Prentice Hall.

Davidson Institute for Talent Development. (n.d.). Programs & scholarships. Retrieved September 10, 2022, from www.davidsongifted.org/

Davidson Institute for Talent Development. (2021). *Mentoring guidebook*. Retrieved from www.davidsongifted.org/wp-content/uploads/2021/03/Davidson_Guidebook_Mentoring_2021.pdf

Johnson, R. (Director). (2017, December 9). *Star wars: The last Jedi* [Film]. Walt Disney Studios Motion Pictures.

Kershner, I. (Director). (1980, May 6). *The empire strikes back* [Film]. 20th Century Fox.

Rogers, K. B. (2002). *Re-forming gifted education: Matching the program to the child*. Great Potential Press, Inc.

Winebrenner, S., & Brulles, D. (2018). *Teaching gifted kids in today's classroom* (4th ed.). Free Spirit Publishing.

Every Sidekick Needs a Hero

The 1985 film *Back to the Future* highlights the significance an individual moment can have in our lives. In the movie, Marty McFly travels to the past and interrupts the moment his parents meet. In doing so, he sets off a chain of events that not only would prevent the meeting from happening but would also mean he is never born. Marty spends the rest of the film trying to recreate the moment his parents fell in love (Zemeckis, 1985). This event he and his siblings thought was a silly story their parents shared was actually the key to their entire existence.

When we think about our pasts, I am sure we can identify many moments that shaped who we are today. Those proverbial forks in the road of life seemed small at the time, but would have a huge impact in where we are today. With many of these events, we can identify the special individuals who made those moments so significant. For example, when I received my student teaching placement, I was placed in a gifted cluster classroom. I did not know at that time that this teacher would change my life. She showed me what it meant to be a great teacher of gifted students and introduced me to the director of gifted education for the district who would later become my mentor. I had no idea in that moment how important that placement was.

Every day our gifted middle schoolers come to school, and their lives are filled with many of these individual moments, both good and bad. They are at an age where the world is not as simple as it seemed, and they are having to deal with a myriad of things before they even step foot inside our classroom. Middle school can be a lonely place, and it can shape so much of what the future will hold. This chapter considers the role we

DOI: 10.4324/9781003332015-11

play in those individual moments, and how we can best support our gifted students so they know they are not alone.

No Educator Is an Island

As we discuss supporting our gifted students' social-emotional needs, it is important to remember that you are not alone. Schools, by design, are made up of different individuals with different specialties, all with the shared purpose of helping students. Your job is not to be a therapist, and you should not feel pressured to guide students in that way. Counselors and other professionals have gone through extensive training, and it is irresponsible to try and assume that role. It is not fair to our students, who might need more focused support, and it is not fair to you, who already has enough responsibility with leading a classroom. It can feel like we need to solve all the problems facing our students alone, but that is simply not true.

One of the benefits of working at a middle school is that there are many stakeholders who are involved in the lives of our students. They are resources who can provide insight, as well as considering ways to help them. Connecting with a counselor or social worker can be especially beneficial in addressing social-emotional concerns. If your school or district does not have a dedicated counselor or social worker, please speak with your administration about how best to support these student needs.

There is also importance in involving parents in these discussions. By connecting with home, it provides a more rounded picture of what is occurring, as well as tapping into all the resources available. A quick five-minute phone call can either alert parents to something concerning or help them know the school is there to support them as well.

I Thought You Were Gifted

Think through your schedule, and across the five or six periods you teach, ask yourself this: what is the feeling of each class?

Our classrooms hold a great deal of significance in the lives of our students. While they are the places where learning happens, they are much more than that. Successes and failures are experienced. New love can bloom or hearts can be broken. Laughter can fill the air or anxiety can leave it quiet. Without us knowing, our classroom takes on its own personality, almost becoming an entity itself. Although these classroom personas will typically happen naturally, given the dynamics of having groups of different students with their own personalities, it is critical that our classrooms are places of safety and trust.

The beginning of this book focused heavily on establishing a positive culture, and it cannot be overstated how important this is. In addition to supporting identity development, creating an environment of safety and trust equips your gifted students to know they do not need to have all the answers. There is a lot of pressure that comes with being identified as gifted, and this pressure can be overwhelming. Imagine being told you have the potential to change the world, but you are struggling with something that seems inconsequential when weighed against the problems facing humanity. That is a difficult place to be.

One of the things we need to establish early with gifted middle schoolers is that it is alright to ask for help. This coincides with the discussions on perfectionism, but we want to establish early ways for students to communicate need. I have talked with many parents who will tell me that their child is struggling with something at home, but does not know how to communicate it. Naturally, the parent steps in to give support, and while I am glad we are able to reach a solution, we want to use these opportunities to develop advocacy skills in the student.

A strategy I recommend with parents is if they are aware of a concern, have their child send me the email instead of them. This simple act can go a long way in opening communication between student and teacher. If a student does not know how to begin writing an email like that, I have recommended that parents and their children write the message together. Even if a parent dictates word-for-word what should be included, having the student initiate communication is an important tool in developing advocacy skills. The hope is that in developing skills in this way, if there is something bigger or more urgent that comes up, the student understands how to get the help they need.

With these communications, it is very important we do not make students feel bad for reaching out for help. Part of establishing a community of trust is that students do not feel like we have judged them or look down on them for asking for support. Every one of the students in our classes should look to us to guide them and support them in both academic and personal ways. Whether we are aware of it or not, everything we do is building and developing a relationship, and gifted students, especially those who demonstrate an intellectual overexcitability, are incredibly perceptive (Sousa, 2009). Our reactions when a student makes a mistake or is struggling can define the relationship for the rest of the school year, and their perceived understanding of our expectations can completely shape a student's academic self-perception (Verhoeven et al., 2019). Comments like "The answer to your question was on the board all week" or "I told you not to procrastinate" do not support our students in growing and communicate to them that they will be judged if they ask for help. Even if they are seeking support for something we have told them dozens of times, our reaction needs not to penalize them for seeking support.

Middle school is a critical time, because, as adolescents get older, the value they place on our relationship becomes more important. As gifted adolescents develop more independence, if there is not a reciprocation of effort, then why should they invest in cultivating the relationship, especially when we are the adult and there are five other teachers with whom they could foster a positive interaction?

What makes this especially difficult, however, is that, as mentioned, gifted students are incredibly observant and sensitive when it comes to interpreting actions. Things we might not expect to have an impact can make a big difference and be a source of pain.

During my unit on *The Outsiders* (Hinton, 2006), I spent most of our class discussions addressing what it means to be gifted with the students. While we would bring the conversations back to the book, this time afforded us an opportunity to connect to the text in an incredibly meaningful way. Throughout the book, one of the big topics that comes up is the pressure Ponyboy feels to live up to his potential, which was a common feeling felt by my class. As we discussed this, one of the students mentioned how their family sometimes made them feel like they were a failure.

I knew this family well, and they were incredibly loving and supportive. The student would often share about their weekend adventures. I knew the love the parents had for their child, so naturally I was surprised to hear this. They went on to explain that it was not school or sports where they felt this way, but rather, with simple tasks. If they were asked to do something and were unable to, the family would give the student a hard time, even joking and saying, "I thought you were gifted."

The intention of those five words was meant as nothing more than a joke, but the impact they had was clear. There was no ill intent with this, as the family regularly interacted in this way, but this student saw it as something more. After they shared, more members of the class expressed similar experiences of how the adults in their lives unintentionally made them feel small. In none of their stories or comments of agreement did they say there was any ill intent, but the result was always the same: they were hurt.

The words we say have power, and our gifted middle schoolers are constantly reading meaning into and dissecting what we say. Little comments or changing the way we interact can have a lasting impact that can completely alter the dynamic in a classroom and change the way our students see us. We typically have one hour each day with our classes and losing trust during that time can be devastating. This can also have an impact on student success.

Students will meet the expectations we set for them. For example, Heyd-Metzuyanim identified how her low expectations of a math student negatively impacted that student's success and self-perception (2013). Conversely, when teachers show they care and believe in their students' potential, they live up to those expectations (Long-Mitchell, 2011). At the core, these studies are emphasizing the role we play beyond our curriculum. Our gifted students need to know we believe in them.

As we work with our middle schoolers, consider the nature of what we say as well as how we say it. Our classes require meaningful and honest feedback to help them grow, but we do not want that messaging to get lost. In everything we do, we should consider the lasting impact and what message it is sending to them

We're Not So Different, You and I

Throughout my career, I have worked almost exclusively with gifted adolescents, and it is easy to lose sight of the struggles they can experience making connections with peers and adults. While there are many incredible aspects of gifted students, with their intense passion and inquisitive minds (Lind, 2011; Sousa, 2009), those same attributes can be a challenge. As teachers, we are trying to do a million things and it can be tiring. For our students, though, those same challenges can make their lives very lonely. In Delisle and Galbraith's *When Gifted Kids Don't Have All the Answers* they identify "The Eight Gripes of Gifted Kids." The fourth gripe they identify is: "Friends who really understand us are few and far between" (Delisle & Galbraith, 2002, p. 155).

The social aspect of middle school cannot be understated, and many of our gifted students are just trying to figure out where they fit in. While identity development is central, this can also result in our gifted students making a lot of mistakes that can alienate both peers and adults.

I think about a student I once had in the gifted self-contained middle school program. Like all my students they were an incredibly creative thinker with a great deal of potential, but their greatest strength was their wit. While they earned good grades, they did not push themself to succeed academically, and instead, chose to distinguish themself through their role of "class clown." Pretty much any time they would share something in class it was a joke, and eventually, this started to seep into their class work. Not only were they not turning in assignments, but they also stopped participating in group activities, acting as more of a disruption than a support. Their grades started to suffer, and they started to alienate their peers who did not want to work with them.

As the year progressed, my teaching partner and I became more frustrated with the disruptions, and eventually pulled them from class to meet. We had had several meetings with parents already, but at this point we were at a loss. We explained our frustrations (something they had heard before), but then my teaching partner asked the student how we could help. What could we do to avoid these disruptions in the future? They were not sure, so she asked them to come the next day with a list of strategies for how we could help them make better choices.

After she stepped out, I took a moment to talk one-on-one with the student, but instead of explaining why I was frustrated or that their behavior was inappropriate, I told them I understood where they were coming from. I explained that I used to be a bit of a class clown myself, and I knew that it was hard to find that line between being a good student and making jokes in class. I concluded by sharing how much I hoped they would find that line, because they had so much potential. The next day my teaching partner and I did not expect them to bring the list we asked for, but sure enough, they had a handwritten list of strategies they thought might help them be more successful.

As we consider our role as supports for gifted middle school students, it is important to realize that role is not defined by expertise or even perfection. So much of middle school is feeling isolated and that can be compounded by being gifted. While teachers train and educate their classes, they also are a comfort and support. Guiding our gifted students moves beyond just one role, and speaks to meeting that child's individual needs, whatever they might be. For some, it is academic support and knowing we believe in them; for others, it is simply knowing we care.

Weight of the World

Think about the challenges facing the world right now.

Depending on when and where you are reading this book, the challenges you identified might be different, but in 2022 in the United States, there are a lot of problems. Even looking back two years, in 2020 there was a global pandemic that split the United States on top of causing millions of deaths worldwide (CDC, 2022), the murder of George Floyd brought protests across the country fighting for an end to racial inequality (History.com Editors, 2021), there was a riot on the U.S. Capitol (History. com Editors, 2022), all on top of growing concerns over global warming, gender inequality, and gun violence. Regardless of where you stand politically on any of these issues, it is crucial that we understand the pressure that our gifted adolescents are feeling.

What makes this especially difficult is the asynchronous nature of gifted children. They tend to have a strong sense of right and wrong, so when there are issues like these facing the world, there is an effort to want to find out more and fix the problem. While our gifted youth can understand the complex nature of much of what they are reading, they are still often processing this information as middle school aged students. This can be a lot to take in, as research does not always paint the most positive image of the future.

I had one student, for example, who struggled a great deal with the idea of global warming. This student spent hours researching what experts had to say, and unfortunately, much of that research said the damage done was irreparable. On top of that, the student saw frequent arguments from the adults in the world on the news, with most of the stories focused on how they were not actively working to fix the problem. This student saw the entire situation as hopeless and struggled to complete work and stay engaged in class.

The stress about feeling powerless in the world is a real concern for gifted adolescents (Delisle & Galbraith, 2002), and something we need to take seriously. One of the ways we can do this is by being active listeners to the concerns that our students have. By acknowledging their feelings and validating their concerns, we help give them a level of respect for what they are experiencing. This allows for follow-up questions to be asked, as well as opportunities to help students find resources or consider perspectives that might take a more active role in finding a solution.

This also bridges into another aspect of supporting our gifted students: when they are concerned about a problem, the answer is to empower them to be solution oriented. By placing the emphasis on finding a solution, it helps to contextualize their concern through realizing that there are people actively working to solve the problems facing the world. While the problems are still present, by understanding the steps being taken, it helps to transform the problem from something inevitable to something they can work to solve as well.

This also connects to the ways in which we present our curriculum. While being dramatic can be a powerful way to gain the students' attention, understanding the social-emotional well-being of our students is critical. I can remember sitting in my 9th grade science class, and my teacher talking about super volcanoes that would destroy all life as we knew it. She closed out that discussion by casually mentioning that the world was long overdue for another and just moved on. As a gifted adolescent this terrified me, and while I did not want my peers to know the stress I was feeling, it was something that stuck in the back of my mind for a good portion of that year. When we introduce problems, I think it is incredibly valuable to couple them with solutions. This does not mean we have to solve all the problems, but rather use this as a platform to empower our gifted students to understand the ways in which we take something concerning and use that to fuel action.

What if I Lose by a Lot?

Although we can work to support our gifted middle schoolers, the reality is, no matter how hard we try, we cannot always keep them from getting hurt. Middle school is a challenging place to navigate, and sometimes, our students will experience things we do not want them to. Friendships will be lost, failures will be experienced, and they will be embarrassed. There will be times when we sit powerless and wish we could help, but in my experience, there is something incredibly powerful we can do: be there for our students through the good and bad.

When I was coaching middle school track, I always encouraged my students to join. Track was a very low-stress sport for students to participate in, as anybody who joined would get the opportunity to participate in two district track meets. It gave the students an opportunity to be involved without needing to compete for a spot- on the team.

During one of the meets, I had a student who was running the 800-meter dash, and they were the only student running from our school. When they called the event, we walked together to the starting line, and the student was unusually quiet. When I asked them what was wrong, they did not look up from the ground. As they avoided eye contact, they said, "What if I lose by a lot?"

In that moment they had already conceded that they were going to lose, and their primary concern was by how much. At this meet there were three different schools represented, and each school brought between 50 and 100 students, so the stands were filled with parents in addition to students. I did not have some secret weapon that would make this student win the race, and I had coached long enough to know where the student's typical time fell in relation to the rest of the runners.

At that moment, all I could do was be there for them. We stopped before they stepped on the track, and I told them, "I don't care if you lose. All I care about is that you try your best to beat your personal best time. That is all you need to worry about."

They ran the race and lost. As the student walked off the track, they looked defeated, and I walked over to them. When I asked them how their personal best compared to the time in which they ran that race, the student, in a tone more defeated than before they ran, said they had shaved over a minute off their best time. When they told me this, I exploded in celebration, and fortunately, a high school volunteer who was walking by heard this and confirmed how amazing an accomplishment that was. I told this student how proud I was of them and went on coaching the rest of the meet. After the competition was done, they ran up to thank me. There was nothing special I did that night; I just let them know that win, lose, or draw, I was there and proud of them.

There are moments that can define an experience and shape the way we see the world. Middle school is filled with times like these, and unfortunately, many of them are hard. Adolescence is an awkward time, and every decision can feel like the wrong one. We can feel powerless as we watch our students struggle and not know how to help them. Throughout this book we have discussed many different strategies for helping gifted middle schoolers, but one of the most important is simply being present.

In the 2012 film *The Dark Knight Rises*, Batman summarizes this idea while talking to Commissioner Gordon. He explains, "A hero can be anyone. Even a man doing something as simple and reassuring as putting a coat around a young boy's shoulders to let him know the world hadn't ended" (Nolan, 2012). Middle school can be an isolating place, but we can show our students they are not alone. Even if we cannot change the circumstances or the outcome, we can still be the hero they need.

Summary

Gifted students can carry the weight of the world on their shoulders. While they can reason and process complex material, due to asynchronous development, they are processing these feelings in line with their age. As a result, these students need support in working through these feelings. One important aspect to supporting gifted middle schoolers is making sure qualified individuals are supporting students to meet their needs. Collaborating with parents and counselors is crucial to making sure students are supported. In addition, framing problems through a solution-oriented lens can help adolescents feel empowered. Despite our best efforts, there will be hardships we cannot prevent our gifted middle schoolers from experiencing. With these situations, it is important that our students know we are there for them, even when things seem their hardest.

Reflection

1. Reflect on a time you were there for a student. What did that student need? How did you know? What did you do to support them?

References

CDC. (2022, August 16). CDC museum COVID-19 timeline. Centers for Disease Control and Prevention. Retrieved from www.cdc.gov/museum/timeline/covid19.html

Delisle, J., & Galbraith, J. (2002). *When gifted kids don't have all the answers*. Free Spirit Publishing.

Heyd-Metzuyanim, E. (2013). The co-construction of learning difficulties in mathematics: Teacher–student interactions and their role in the development of a disabled mathematical identity. *Educational Studies in Mathematics*, *83*(3), 341–368. https://doi.org/10.1007/s10649-012-9457-z

Hinton, S. E. (2006). *The outsiders*. Viking Books for Young Readers.

History.com Editors. (2021, June 25). George Floyd is killed by a police officer, igniting historic protests. HISTORY. Retrieved from www.history.com/this-day-in-history/george-floyd-killed-by-police-officer

History.com Editors. (2022, June 9). U.S. Capitol riot. HISTORY. Retrieved from www.history.com/this-day-in-history/january-6-capitol-riot

Lind, S. (2011, September 14). Overexcitability and the gifted. SENG. Retrieved from www.sengifted.org/post/overexcitability-and-the-gifted

Long-Mitchell, L. (2011). High-achieving Black adolescents' perceptions of how teachers impact their academic achievement. In J. A. Castellano & A. D. Frazier (Eds.), *Special populations in gifted education: Understanding our most able students from diverse backgrounds*. Prufrock Press Inc.

Nolan, C. (Director). (2012, July 16). *The dark knight rises* [Film]. Warner Bros. Pictures.

Sousa, D. A. (2009). *How the gifted brain learns* (2nd ed.). Corwin.

Verhoeven, M., Poorthuis, A. M. G., & Volman, M. (2019). The role of school in adolescents' identity development: A literature review. *Educational Psychology Review*, *31*(1), 35–63. https://doi.org/10.1007/s10648-018-9457-3

Zemeckis, R. (Director). (1985, July 3). *Back to the future* [Film]. Universal Pictures.

Conclusion

I have read a lot of comic books, and, while I always enjoy the spectacle that comes with caped heroes fighting villains, some of my favorite Superman comics are not focused on an epic battle, but rather, are the ones where he inspires others to stand up for what is right. Although Superman can fly and shoot lasers from his eyes, one of his greatest powers is the way he makes others feel about themselves.

Most of this book has focused on our gifted middle schoolers, but in this last section, I want to shift the focus. Every day, *you* return to a grade level that most people would hate to revisit. I have seen countless parents terrified at the thought that their child will experience what they once did and are desperate for any guidance. *You* support students and parents at a critical moment that is one of the most vulnerable times any of us have experienced. Middle school is not just another grade; it is a pivotal time that can shape a child's future, for better or for worse.

You might be wondering about the impact you make, as the proof can be hard to see, but trust me: you are making a difference.

I wrote this book because I saw a need. In the greater span of key formative educational years, middle school is regularly overlooked, and for gifted students, this can be a time when they specifically do not have their needs addressed. Whether these are academic and/or social-emotional, gifted students can get lost in this challenging and confusing time.

DOI: 10.4324/9781003332015-12

While it is easy to view middle school as a time to figure out things before high school, please never lose sight of the value this time has in the lives of our gifted students. This period is so unique, as our students start to discover who they are, and what the future might hold. Most will make mistakes, but fortunately, they will have you to help guide them.

You teach middle school … thank you!

Appendix
"Fun" Attendance Questions

The following list is broken into different categories to provide questions that fit a variety of scenarios. As you get to understand your students and classes better, you will know which questions they connect with and which they do not. Please use the following lists as inspiration to create your own!

Open-Ended

These questions give students the most freedom and voice in their responses and can be the most illuminating. While these questions can take up a bit of class time, it is valuable to let students have the time to think and process what they want to say. Typically, if a student is stuck on what they want to say, I will give them time to think and return later. If these questions take up too much of your class time, consider only using them on Fridays as a fun way to close out the week.

Open-Ended Questions

- What is your favorite road trip snack?
- What is one song you would add to a road trip playlist?
- If you could have lunch with any historical figure, who would it be?
  - You can substitute historical figure with literary character, celebrity, etc.

- If the principal were to buy the class lunch, where would you like it to be ordered from?
- What is your favorite song?
- Who is your favorite musician/band?
- What is your favorite movie?
- If you could live in any fictional universe, what would it be?
- You are told you can only take one item with you on a long trip. If all necessities are covered (food, clothing, toiletries, etc.), what would you take with you?
- What is one thing you plan to do over the weekend?
- If you could learn any language, what language would you want to learn?
- If you could have any superpower, what superpower would it be?
- What is your favorite book?
- If you could travel in time, what is the first thing you would do?
- What is a treat that reminds you of childhood?
  - This is always a funny question to ask, as you can see their perspective being teenagers.

Weird Open-Ended Questions

I made a separate section for "Weird Questions" because, as the name implies, they can be quite odd. When I ask students questions like these, I will typically get several confused stares, but they usually result in a great deal of laughter, fun, and creativity. With questions like these, be aware that students can get highly distracted by what is being asked (I still have students debating how they think a spider would wear pants).

- If a spider were to wear pants, how would it wear them? On the back legs or across all eight legs?
  - You can replace spider with any quadruped animal with this question. I had a class who got really invested in the discussion of spiders, so I wanted to include it.

- If your hair were replaced with pasta, not including spaghetti, angel hair, or other similar pasta varieties, what type of noodle would you like your hair to be replaced with?
- Without sharing the question, give me the answer to the question you think I should ask.
  - When I am at a loss for an attendance question, my students will usually jump in with suggestions. This is always a fun prompt, as you will jump from students saying Batman, to those saying chocolate-covered strawberries, and Lebron James without any context.
- What is your lame superpower?
  - I usually prompt this attendance question by explaining to my students that it would be unfortunate to get superpowers but find out your power was something along the lines of being able to smell better than the average person.
- Add an ingredient to a salad that should not or does not belong, but works.

Would You Rather…

"Would You Rather" questions are effective to use in the classroom, as these provide students with limited options. They can move through the attendance list quicker, while still giving students an option to have fun. In doing this type of attendance questions with gifted students, be prepared for them to try and add a third choice to the list. Before beginning the attendance, I will typically preface the choices by explaining that these are the only two options available.

- Would you rather…
  - live in the mountains or at the beach?
  - be able to speak any language or play any instrument?
  - be a pirate or a ninja?
  - be the best player on the worst team or the worst player on the best team?
  - go to the Super Bowl or to the concert of your favorite band?

- be able to see 30 seconds into the future or travel back in time 30 seconds?
- compete in the Olympics or have written a best-selling novel?
- be able to turn invisible or read minds?
- have a soup or salad with your meal?
- always be 15 minutes late or always arrive 30 minutes early?
- own a cat or a dog?
- have cake or ice cream?
- go to the museum or the aquarium?
- be able to have a conversation with a whale or an eagle?
- have shoelaces that are constantly untied or a scratchy tag on your shirt?

Content-Based Questions

The attendance questions can connect to what is being learned in class, and even reinforce concepts you want students to consider. I do not typically spend too much time using questions like these, but when I do, they are usually fun extensions of what we are learning.

- On a scale of 1–10, how would you rate the book we just read?
  - I have used this rating system after studies of novels in literature, and the answers are always fascinating. Students whom I did not expect to love a particular book do, and others who were really engaged in discussions really have disliked the same novel. This question gives you insight into student likes and dislikes, and allows meaningful content decisions to be made for the future. It is important, though, to make sure students know they are entitled to their perspectives, and you want them to be honest with their ratings.
- What punctuation mark best describes you?
- Give an example of one of the parts of speech.
- Describe your favorite holiday without saying its name.
- What element on the periodic table best represents you?

- If you were any part of the cell, which part would you be?
- If you could have lunch with any historical figure, who would you choose?
- What is the greatest invention in human history?

Class Stories

This style of attendance question involves the biggest time commitment, but they can also push student creativity. By providing the first line to a story, each student adds a line with the goal of telling a completed tale with a beginning, middle, and end. I always set clear expectations with these stories: they must be school appropriate, students cannot end the world or completely disregard the existing story, or have the story end with "…and it was all a dream."

- Jenna's life was always mundane until she opened the refrigerator.
- Danny never considered how much he could eat, but there he was, in the middle of a pie-eating contest.
- All the stores in the mall were closed … except for one.
- Who would have thought finding the lottery numbers would be so easy?
- Nobody expected to love the cafeteria soup, but there was a line for seconds.

For Product Safety Concerns and Information please contact our EU
representative GPSR@taylorandfrancis.com
Taylor & Francis Verlag GmbH, Kaufingerstraße 24, 80331 München, Germany

www.ingramcontent.com/pod-product-compliance
Ingram Content Group UK Ltd.
Pitfield, Milton Keynes, MK11 3LW, UK
UKHW021433080625
459435UK00011B/252

* 9 7 8 1 0 3 2 3 6 3 6 8 4 *